The 7 Essentials for Lasting Success

To Achieve Grand Goals
These Are Not Optional

Revised Edition

The 7 Essentials for Lasting Success

Copyright 2025

Sherry Buffington, Ph.D.

    All rights reserved. No part of this publication may be reproduced, stored in any retrieval system, or transmitted in any form or by any means, mechanical, photocopying, recording, or otherwise, without permission in writing from the publisher, except by a reviewer, who may quote brief passages in a review to be printed in a magazine or newspaper.

Cover Design: Sherry Buffington

Edited by: Gina Morgan

Manufactured in the United States of America

ISBN: 978-0-9708926-2-1

QuinStar Publishing – Lawrence, KS

Acknowledgement

With endless love and appreciation I want to acknowledge the great contributions my daughter, business partner, best friend, editor, and sanity-saver, Gina Morgan, has made to this book. Her keen eye, wisdom, wordsmithing, and design talent has immensely improved this book.

Thank you my brilliant, talented daughter! I love you!

Contents

Introduction 1

CHAPTER ONE - The Primary Driver 9

CHAPTER TWO - The Perfect Guidance System 13

CHAPTER THREE - Essential Number One
Authentic Self-Awareness & Expression 25

CHAPTER FOUR - Essential Number Two
Clear Purpose & Focus 39

CHAPTER FIVE - Essential Number Three
Open, Expectant Attitude and Beliefs 47

CHAPTER SIX - Essential Number Four
Solid Personal & Relationship Boundaries 53

CHAPTER SEVEN - Essential Number Five
Self-Confidence 63

CHAPTER EIGHT - Essential Number Six
Self-Esteem 67

CHAPTER NINE - Essential Number Seven
Effective Self-Management 73

CHAPTER TEN - Creating Your Path to Success 79

CHAPTER ELEVEN - Wrapping It All Up 97

If You Need More Help 102

About the Author 104

*Do not go where the path may lead.
Go instead where there is no path
... and leave a trail.*

Ralph Waldo Emerson

Introduction
Discovering the Seven Essentials

How do you react when you read or hear statements such as, "Whatever the mind can conceive and believe, it can achieve" or "Opportunity for the acquisition of wealth is as plentiful as the air we breathe"? Your reaction says far more about you than about the accuracy of the statement.

The first statement was made by Napoleon Hill in his perennially popular book *Think and Grow Rich*. The second one was made by W. Clement Stone in his popular book *The Success System That Never Fails*. When I first read these statements back in the early eighties, my response was, "Yeah, right!" I responded that way because I had read both books multiple times, plus hundreds of others. I knew all the principles espoused in these books and had tried with all my might to make them work for me. In the struggle to succeed I had discovered that you can't just think and grow rich. And though I conceded that it might be true that "*opportunity* for the acquisition of wealth is as plentiful as air," I had learned that getting access to such opportunities was nowhere near as easy as getting access to air.

Hill presents thirteen success principles in *Think and Grow Rich* which are closely mirrored in Stone's *The Success System That Never Fails*. Jack Canfield's book, *The Success Principles*, has sixty-seven! Canfield's book is much more comprehensive, but most people give up long before mastering enough of them to make a difference. Like most authors of success principles, these well-read authors assure readers that, if they follow the principles they present in their book, they *will* succeed and gain the wealth, riches and lifestyle they desire.

Although some people swear by the principles presented in such books, for most people the promises don't pan out. Why is that? It was this question that set me on a twenty-five year odyssey to find the answer.

Have you ever wondered why so few people succeed on a grand scale while most people continue to struggle? Do you wonder why so many are not enjoying happiness, health, wealth, great relationships, fit bodies and overall abundance when there are tens of thousands of books, audio programs, workshops, weekend retreats, and other products on the market that claim to teach people how to be successful in every area of life? True success is more than just wealth. Think about people who seem to "have it all" but still struggle because money or fame in and of themselves don't bring satisfaction.

Since the start of the twentieth century there has been an almost limitless supply of products in the marketplace explaining how to achieve every kind of success. These days it isn't even necessary to take the time or effort to read. You just que up an audio file, sit back and listen. There are even subliminal programs that claim to alter the mind and create automatic change so you don't even have to think! All you have to do, these programs claim, is listen to pleasant music and you will be magically transformed.

Every year millions of people invest a lot of time, effort and money in these products and programs without ever coming close to getting the results promised.

Have you ever wondered exactly what it is that separates those who are highly successful from those who work very hard, struggling to improve their circumstances, but never managing to arrive? I have pondered this deeply, which is why I dedicated twenty-five years to finding the answer. I began this quest to understand why, in spite of the fact that I was working very hard and spending every spare moment studying everything I could get my hands on, I continued to struggle and to fall short of the level of success I so longed to experience.

I had observed with some consternation that most successful people didn't seem to work nearly as hard as I worked. They had time to enjoy life, family and friends, to travel and see the world, stay fit, relax, and do all sorts of things that people who were struggling, like I was at the time, didn't have the time or energy to do. The successful clearly weren't working harder, so obviously hard work was *not* the answer.

As it turns out, the amount of time and money invested is not the deciding factor either. Neither is the desire for achieving a good outcome. Those who are unsuccessful yearn for a healthy bank account and the free time to enjoy life just as much as the wealthy. They want the advantages of wealth just as much as those who have them.

Most seekers have invested time and money in dozens of things hoping to find something that actually works. Many stick with a program for months or even years before they give up and go in search of another solution. And every new beginning is filled with the hope that *this time* they will find the road to success.

At some point, it becomes apparent that the new path they have chosen is not getting them the result they desire either, so they abandon that path and go off in search of still another—and the cycle starts all over again.

We marvel at people who grew up in poverty, never got much of an education, have physical handicaps or other challenges and still become highly successful. Those who make it to the top with apparent ease in spite of starting out with few visible advantages have a lot to teach us if we are looking in the right places, but most of the information out there on achieving success doesn't point us in the direction we need to go *first*.

Among the questions I set out in 1984 to try to answer were, "What is it that allows ordinary and even apparently disadvantaged people to rise to the top when there are so many people with far greater advantages that continue to struggle?" "What factors drive those who experience true success and what allows them to maintain the successes they have achieved over time?" "If the principles and practices typically presented in success products and programs actually work, why do so many people who diligently study and apply them keep struggling?"

I began interviewing people who had gained and maintained success in spite of having ordinary and sometimes very difficult beginnings. I interviewed people who had created financial success in business as entrepreneurs. I interviewed successful leaders and top producing salespeople. I interviewed people who had excelled in sports, people who had lost a lot of weight and kept it off, people who had increased their fitness level and maintained it, people who had created and maintained happy, successful relationships, and people who exuded personal power and joy.

Many were unable to tell me what they did differently from others. They could share their philosophies, talk about their values and explain what they did or did not do in the external world, but few were able to directly answer the one question I most wanted answered; "What is it that drives you; that keeps you doing the things you do such that you have been able to achieve and maintain your success?"

Where some pointed to a great home life and supportive parents, others spoke of difficult beginnings and disconnected parents. Where some knew early in life what they wanted to do and be, others felt lost and undirected well into adulthood. Where some went from under-achiever to "overnight" success from one flash of insight, for others the rise to success was a slow, gradual process.

All were able to point to a catalyst that set them on their path, but their experiences differed. For some it was a defining moment which caused something to shift in them immediately such that they were no longer willing to continue down an unproductive or unhealthy path. For others there were more subtle shifts.

I wanted to understand the catalyst, but few could explain what had changed them. After hundreds of interviews, patterns in their answers began to emerge. One thing that became apparent was that they all took complete responsibility for their outcomes and stepped up to the plate, but a lot of unsuccessful people do that too. I kept looking.

I found that all successful people were doing things they were passionate about and enjoyed doing. Some unsuccessful people are doing that too, but there was a difference here. Successful people didn't let unimportant things rob them of time or dilute their energy, where moderately successful people sometimes did, and unsuccessful people often did. I knew there had to be some underlying attribute the| successful people had and finding it became part of my research.

The most successful were very clear about what they wanted and were willing to apply themselves to getting it. Many spoke of the dedication and persistence it took to reach the pinnacle, but none saw the effort it took to get there as hard work. As with the ability to stick with what's important and ignore distractions, I knew there had to be an underlying factor which allowed persistent effort to seem effortless. I wanted to know what it was that allowed highly successful people to sustain their momentum, when for the masses momentum tended to fade after a short time. And I wanted to know why there was no obvious resistance to the effort and dedication they described.

For the most part, beyond pointing to the passion they felt for what they were doing, the deeper questions went unanswered. Then one day I posed the "What drives you?" question to my son, Randall, who had just graduated from the University of Kansas with honors. This was a young man who barely squeaked through high school and had dropped out of college years earlier. At the age of twenty-three he announced that he was going back to school and this time would excel. In fact, he announced, he planned to be a straight "A" student.

With his poor academic record, I felt his goal was a little ambitious, but encouraged him to try. I expressed my concern only by suggesting that he not allow less-than-perfect grades to deter him. His reply to my suggestion was "Mom, I am going to be an 'A' student. I won't settle for less."

Not only did he meet that grand goal, he graduated at the top of his class and received the Senior of the Year award at graduation. When I asked Randall what had changed for him, what shifted him from a kid just drifting along to a successful graduate with a world of promise, he thought for a minute and replied, "I was able to do it because you always believed in me—and then I found that Proctor believed in me too."

Proctor was Randall's employer before he returned to school. Proctor contracted polio at the age of thirty-three and was paralyzed, yet was a very successful building contractor. Randall was Proctor's personal aid and as such, had become very close to him. They shared many deep and meaningful conversations. Seeing that a man in a wheelchair, crippled by a disease, could still be highly successful undoubtedly influenced Randall's thinking. But I couldn't see what I had to do with the shift he experienced. I had always believed in Randall's abilities and he knew it, so I was not convinced that my faith in him was part of the equation and continued to probe.

After several questions on my part and much contemplation on his, Randall eventually got to self-esteem. I had set the stage, he told me, by always believing in him. But being his mother, he assumed I was biased.

My faith in him was validated by Proctor's faith in him. Proctor had also modeled how one could move beyond adversity to excel. The whole package added up to Randall seeing and believing in greater possibilities and gaining real faith in his ability to succeed. From a place of faith in self, or self-confidence, came the belief that he could do a lot better. The shift occurred, he told me, when he decided that he was *worth the effort!*

Randall went on to receive a Ph.D. in biology from the University of California at Berkeley, and I went back to interviewing successful people with a new awareness and a new set of questions to ask.

Now I wanted to know what role self-esteem (believing you are worth the effort) had in realizing success. From the answers of earlier interviews, I knew that self-awareness, the drive that comes from passion, clarity and self-confidence were present in all successful people, but I had not inquired specifically about the role of self-esteem.

It took me another six years of interviewing and pondering the answers to discover the other essential factors for exceptional success; what they are, how and why they develop, why so many people fail to get the results they desire, and what has to be present for true success (a sense of overall wellbeing and satisfaction) to occur and be lasting.

Seven qualities emerged; qualities which all truly successful people have in common and which appear to be absolutely *essential* for *sustained* success. I found that, to the degree any of the seven were missing or undeveloped, success was limited and often short lived.

Once it was clear that these seven qualities were always present in truly successful people, and I could find no others which were present in all cases, I began searching for ways to help people develop the seven qualities as quickly and effectively as possible.

Everyone Can Succeed

I believe that every normally functioning person has what it takes to succeed. The reason success eludes most people is because they are going about it backwards. They are doing the equivalent of trying to make a computer perform functions for which there is no appropriate software.

Like those who design computers, the designers of success programs tend to assume that you already have the right software and all you need is to increase your speed and processing capabilities. But, just as you can have the fastest computer on the planet with endless processing capabilities and still not get good results if you don't have the right software, you can work as hard and fast as is humanly possible and still not get the results you want if you don't have the right stuff inside.

Without the essential qualities, all the great potential an individual possesses and all their capacity to excel and succeed remain largely untapped.

Like a powerful super-computer, your brain has almost limitless processing power, but your brain is just the hardware. It's the "software" that runs the show. The software is made up of subconscious programs, natural traits and talents, values, beliefs, attitude, capacity, and motivators. It is these that drive or delay action and, unless they support your conscious desires, success will elude you.

It doesn't matter how simple or how comprehensive the principles, practices and strategies for success people study are, unless they have the right stuff inside first, little to nothing will change.

Because we are taught to look outside ourselves for answers, those trying to improve their outcomes tend to keep gathering information hoping to eventually find the answers they are looking for, and most of the people developing success programs keep presenting external ways to achieve it.

Most people, especially lifelong seekers, don't need more information. What they need is a way to unlock all their potential and that happens inside, not in the outer world. The effect of doing the internal work is external success to be sure but, as so many who have tried without success have discovered, we cannot *start* on the outside. As it turns out, we cannot start just anywhere on the inside either. There is a particular starting point and order of progression that culminates in true and lasting success.

With the essential internal qualities developed, all the knowledge you have gathered over the years, all the skills you have gained, all the abilities nature endowed you with, and all the passion you need to propel you forward to success are yours. With access to powerful inner resources, the external actions necessary to achieve outer success develop quickly and almost effortlessly.

Whatever you can do, or dream you can, begin it. Boldness has genius, power and magic in it.

~Goethe~

CHAPTER ONE
The Primary Driver

If you are not experiencing the degree of success, joy and contentment you desire, there is no question that you have abilities that you have not tapped into. Few people are living up to their potential and there are lots of reasons why. Most of the reasons come under the category of conditioning.

Before we are born, we respond to internal and external sounds and to the chemical changes that occur in our mother's body. Anxious mothers tend to produce anxious babies. Happy mothers tend to produce happy babies. Early bird mothers tend to produce early bird babies and night owl mothers usually beget little night owls.

Healthy babies are born to well-nourished mothers. Addicted babies are born to addicted mothers. There is even evidence that the children of women who smoked heavily during pregnancy are more likely to begin smoking early and become heavy smokers. But, the womb is just the beginning in more ways than one. Just as most of our physical growth and development takes place outside the womb, so too does most of our conditioning.

We come into the world hard-wired for many of our attributes; height, hair, skin and eye color on the outside and with predispositions to all kinds of internal factors, not the least of which is personality traits. If we are born into an environment where our natural traits can develop fully and effectively, we reach adulthood prepared for exactly the kind of success we want to experience. *Fully and effectively developed* are the operative words here. Most of us are not born into conditions that allow our natural traits to develop fully and effectively. More often than not we experience conditions that hide our truth from us and lock up our potential.

Most conditioning occurs because of the primary human need to belong; to be accepted and valued by the members of our clan. What we consider our clan can be anything from our immediate family to classmates and friends, members of our church, and the community, town, state, country, or culture. Our clan is whatever group or groups with which we identify and which are significant to us in some way.

There is a biological wisdom in gaining clan acceptance because, prior to societies with rules designed to protect its citizens, only those who were accepted by their clan were cared for and only those who were cared for survived infancy and the inexperience of youth.

Because being valued and accepted are primary drivers, we begin very early in life responding as much or more to the mental and emotional states of others as we do to our own physical needs and desires. We are so easily conditioned because humans, especially in youth, are very malleable. It is this high degree of malleability or adaptability that has made the human species so successful. Combined with our need to be accepted, it has also led to a lot of pain and loss of potential.

Until around age two, we don't recognize ourselves as separate from others so their response to us is what defines us in those first two years. It's the realization that we are our own person, separate from mom and dad, and the desire to be independent that triggers the "terrible twos." By age three most children have already learned that they must adjust their behaviors. Some conform to expectations to gain acceptance. Others learn to manipulate their family to get their way. Still others continue to rebel and deal with the consequences so long as they don't include out and out rejection. However we go about it, behaviors are adjusted to fit expectations - our own or those of others.

An example is expected gender behaviors. Even before age three, children have figured out that there are different expectations for boys than there are for girls. By age three gender roles are firmly established for most children, and by age four most have also figured out what their role within the family dynamic must be.

Around age ten children generally become more concerned with the opinions of their friends and peers than of their families, and it is at this point that they decide what the world expects from them and how they must show up to meet those expectations. In other words, most of us have decided who we are and what life is about by the time we are *ten years old*. For most people, the world view they adopted around age ten remains intact for life. Once our self-concept and world view is established, only an event that has an effect so emotionally significant as to cause us to back up and rethink our position can alter our thinking.

In effect, who most people believed they were at ten is not too far from who they still believe they are as adults. And, as you might imagine, more often than not, that belief is quite flawed.

The result of reaching adulthood with flawed information is an abiding uncertainty; a nagging feeling that something is missing, and we don't know what. We don't know because what's missing is the authentic self that had to be suppressed in early childhood in order to be accepted, valued, and included.

For many adults, the authentic self has been suppressed so completely and for so long that there is now no conscious awareness of it. Early personality research suggests 54% of the general population identify with their conditioned self and believe that the false self, no matter how uncomfortable or ineffective it may be, is their *real* self. Decades of focused research with thousands of subjects indicates that the effects of conditioning adversely impacts more than 84% of people and may skew profile results on single dimensional assessments.

The nagging feeling that something is missing or personal discontent are indicators that the real self is not recognized or being allowed to express. Our greatest capabilities express through our authentic self and, when it's suppressed, people are unable to reach their full potential. Usually, they don't even know what it is. They are compelled to keep searching for that missing *something*, rarely guessing that what's missing is their *true self*.

Authentic self-awareness is the foundation of all success, and the first essential quality we will explore. It's the platform upon which all the other qualities rest and develop. The seven essential qualities are inner resources which open the door to all the knowledge you already have, giving you the outer resources to create successes which are large, lasting and perfectly suited to you.

In these pages I have provided you with a number of exercises to help you explore deeper and discover more, and I have provided resources to help you get past any blocks you may encounter faster and easier. Some are available online for free and some are available only through the organization I co-founded, Quantum Leap University. All are here to help you succeed.

So, let's get started. The life you dream of living awaits you.

Many people are tempted by ego's promise of greatness, never realizing that it is tempting them with something they already own.
~Sherry Buffington~

CHAPTER TWO
The Perfect Guidance System

Over two thousand years ago, the Greek philosopher, Aristotle, observed, *"Happiness is the meaning and the purpose of life, the whole aim and end of human existence."* Years of research into what motivates people and drives outcomes has convinced many researchers, including me, that Aristotle's observation was correct.

We are motivated to change for just two reasons: to move away from pain or toward pleasure. In either case, the goal is a sense of physical, mental, emotional or spiritual well-being—in other words, happiness.

Since 1978 my entire focus has been on creating tools and systems to help people achieve the state Aristotle, called *Eudaimonia. Eudaimonia* is the Greek term for an ideal state where we feel happy, satisfied, confident and capable, and have an overall sense of well-being and success.

Mihaly Csikszentmihalyi (pronounced chick-sent-me-high), a psychologist and distinguished professor of psychology and management at Claremont Graduate University, and author of *Flow: The Psychology of Optimal Experience*, calls this ideal state of being "flow" and has done volumes of research around the correlation between happiness and success.

Csikszentmihalyi, describes flow as "being completely involved in an activity for its own sake. The ego falls away. Time flies. Every action, movement, and thought follows inevitably from the previous one, like playing jazz. Your whole being is involved, and you're using your skills to the utmost."

Flow is commonly described as like being carried by a current, spontaneous, effortless. You forget time. You are free to just go with the flow because you feel sure you can control the situation as necessary. What you are doing feels effortless and yet there is deep concentration and skill that leads to high accomplishment as well as high satisfaction.

Flow is our natural state when we are functioning from our authentic self and have effectively developed our natural attributes. It is easy to see how success would evolve from this delightful place.

Csikszentmihalyi found that flow is a combination of enjoyment and the achievement of excellence, and, like Aristotle, postulated that these are central goals which drive success. Though many use external markers to determine excellence, in flow, it isn't determined by outward appearances as much as by how the individual feels about the outcome. Both Aristotle and Csikszentmihalyi suggest that this high level satisfaction is the reason for anything any of us ever does.

Years of research, and even more years of helping people break free of mental and emotional blocks and develop their potential, bears this thesis out. Most people make huge and lasting shifts that positively impact every area of their life when they get the pleasure/excellence equation right. It is the quest for that perfect combination of pleasure and excellence; reaching our highest potential in the way best suited to our nature, that keeps us all searching until we find it.

Unaware that nature provides each of us with a flawless inner-compass that provides completely dependable guidance, most people search harder than they need to.

The reason so many people are not aware of this flawless guidance system is because it informs us through *feelings*, not through thoughts, and far too many people are not in touch with their feelings.

Men, especially, tend to discount their feelings. They are often taught from an early age to suppress feelings so examining them can be downright scary at first. Many men just refuse to do it, never realizing they are suppressing the finest human guidance system on earth. Even if their parents didn't teach them to avoid their feelings, most men still got that message from their peers, teachers, society, bosses, and the relentlessly biased messages projected in media.

Many large corporations encourage both men and women to suppress their feelings. The message people get in such companies is, "You are expected to get the job done and get it right—leave your emotions at home."

Left-brain logic is prized and emotions discouraged in many school systems too, so getting caught in the logic trap is quite easy. But, thoughts can lead us astray, where feelings never do if we are attending to them properly.

Feelings lead us astray only when we are allowing the immature ones, which filter through emotion rather than logic, to guide us. Generally, if we follow problematical feelings back to their source, we discover that thoughts are driving and distorting them.

Fear, for example, is a natural feeling response and is very useful in the face of danger. Valid fears arise around actual threats, rather than perceived ones. When a threat is perceived, our natural fight, flight or freeze survival response keeps us out of harm's way. The purpose of fear is to ensure our survival and, where it is properly applied, it *never* creates a problem. In fact, properly applied, it always keeps us out of harm's way.

The same cannot be said for thought-produced fears or subconscious triggers which are usually neither valid nor useful. In fact, they create all kinds of problems for us. Invalid fears are fears that have nothing to do with physical survival. When they come up, we respond to them as though we, or those we care about, are in danger when that is, in fact, *not* the case.

The fear response becomes a problem when our thoughts erroneously lead our alert system to report danger in perfectly safe or neutral situations. Say, for instance, you enjoy and really care about people, but are shy. A good friend invites you to a large party and you accept the invitation to please your friend, but won't know anyone else there. The closer the party gets, the more fearful you become. The more fearful you become, the more you don't want to go. If the fear mounts high enough, you will call your friend and make an excuse for not going even though, at some level, you would like to go.

This is an invalid fear response and it was created by your *thoughts*, not the reality. The reality is that it is highly unlikely that there is any real danger lurking at a party put together by friends of your friend. No one is likely to harm or kill you. It could happen, of course, but the odds are so miniscule that fear is inappropriate. So why is there fear where no danger lurks? You are attending to *thoughts*.

Here's how that scenario generally plays out:
- Your past experience tells you that you are not adept at meeting new people and you know the party will be full of them.
- You envision yourself sitting in a corner miserable or, worse yet, you envision someone coming over to talk to you, and you fumbling over your words and looking like an idiot.
- Your subconscious mind takes this worst case scenario and runs with it.

The self-talk or thought process goes something like this: "If I go to the party, I won't know anyone there except my friend. She will get busy with other people and I will be left all alone. People will see how miserable I am, which would be embarrassing. Some of them may feel sorry for me and try to strike up a conversation and, if that happens, I will fall flat of my face like I always do. I am terrible at small talk so I might say something stupid and look like a complete fool. I might be *rejected* or *ridiculed* and, even if I weren't, I would be *embarrassed*. I might even embarrass my friend, and that would be *awful*."

This process, called "awfulizing" always creates a fear response that can shut us down. The reason is because the subconscious mind takes that information and attaches it to the primary human need of being accepted by our clan.

In every age children have depended on their family for food, shelter and validation, and they quickly discover that they get rejected (or disapproved of) when they do "awful" things. If the subconscious mind believes that rejection means our clan will not take care of us, which it apparently does, then *rejection equals death.*

The subconscious mind is very literal and quite illogical. It is also very efficient. It conserves energy by forming habits and by generalizing experiences so we no longer have to think about an action. We just automatically respond. One effect of generalization is the fear response to an evaluation that an action would lead to something awful. The subconscious mind acts on any information it receives, real or imagined, so if our thoughts are taking us to an "*awful*" outcome—and *awful equals death*—then fear is appropriate. Only by becoming aware of the *thoughts* and questioning them, can we get past them and attend to our feelings.

Same Scenario – Different Angle:

- Being aware of your *feelings*, you notice that you are feeling fearful, so you check that response for validity.
- You ask yourself whether your life or the life of someone else will be endangered if you attend the party, and the answer is "no."
- Realizing that the inappropriate *feeling* is driven by *thoughts*, you begin to attend to your *thoughts* to get to a legitimate *feeling*.
- You follow your thoughts back to "that would be *awful*." Now you have the power to re-choose and can create a new scenario. Remember, your subconscious mind acts on whatever information you give it—real or imagined.
- Now imagine that in re-choosing your thoughts, you decide to set a goal to meet two new people at the party and decide it doesn't matter how the meetings turn out. If you meet two new people, you will have achieved your goal and been successful. If the meetings turn out good, you will be doubly successful, but even if they turn out bad, you decide you will use the experience to *learn something* about how to approach and talk to people.
- You then decide that if you do this enough times, you will eventually learn to meet people effectively, which you consider a desirable outcome. So you see the party as an opportunity to improve your relationship skills.
- From this perspective, going to the party has a purpose and you have a mission. Notice that the feelings in relation to *this* thought process are empowering, not fear producing. By attending to the *feeling* and examining the validity of the *thoughts* that have produced it, you are able to choose better responses and get better outcomes. If we paid more attention to feelings, which can sometimes be very subtle, we would make wrong decisions far less frequently.

To add another example, put yourself back at that party. This time:

- You have arrived and are ready to carry out your plan to meet two new people.
- You see someone you are attracted to, and who you want to get to know.

- Still attending to your *feelings*, you become aware of the desire to meet this person as your mind sums up data.
- The person looks right, acts right, and has the right tone of voice so you approach him.
- As you talk with this person, you surmise that he/she seems honest, or kind, or sensual, or whatever it is you find appealing.
- BUT, along with the positive points you are tallying, you become aware that there are also things that don't seem quite right. Red flags are going up all over the place; flags that warn "Be careful! There are things here you need to be concerned about."

How Thoughts Derail Feelings

Imagine that the red flags are going up, but the other person seems interested in you and you want to continue to build this relationship. It is at this point that *thinking* takes over and you stop paying attention to those subtle *feelings* that are telling you to walk away.

Because conscious logic has now taken over, you manage to convince yourself that the good points you see in this person are enough and the flags (which are pure feeling) are ignored. Never mind that there are things that could become a problem in the future. For now, you decide they can be ignored and you forge ahead.

After a relationship has gone sour, people frequently report that there were red flags from the beginning, but they chose to ignore them. When we ignore our feelings, the thoughts always win out, and all too often we are sorry they did.

Another example of thoughts leading people astray would be that of rushing down still another path just like the ones already tried and abandoned, searching for a way to be successful the next time.

People who get caught up in the promises of multi-level or network marketing programs only to lose interest and drop out—again and again—are examples of this. There is nothing wrong with network marketing, mind you. Those suited to it can do quite well. I'm talking about the hundreds of thousands of people who sign up for multi-level marketing programs and never succeed with them; those who keep changing products and programs always assuming that a different product, or price, or up-line will work.

In this case, the thinking is that *this* MLM might have a better product or program or price point; or the people who sponsor them might be more helpful. Perhaps they think a different product or service might be easier to sell than the products in the other multi-level programs. Or maybe they buy into the idea that selling won't be necessary. Maybe they think a better profit margin, or a program that is better structured, or an up-line that is more dedicated to helping their down-line will lead to success. The point is, they are all *thoughts;* rationalizations.

If an individual rushing down a similar path for the umpteenth time were to consult their *feelings*, they would get a whole different story. Their feelings are likely conveying that this endeavor, like the others, is about the promise of easy money, not passion; that liking a product well enough to use it is not the same as liking it enough to sell it, or to build a down-line to sell it.

The *feelings* are likely conveying that this new endeavor doesn't fit any more than the last ones did. That it's the *process*, not the products, prices, program, people or company that doesn't fit. The feedback from the *feelings* would likely be doubt or a sense that one should wait and not get caught up in the heat of the moment again. The feelings usually become obvious a few days or weeks later, but they were there on *day one*, and would have been just as obvious had they been consulted.

Those same gnawing feelings appear when we are off our authentic path. We feel frustrated, insecure, doubtful, worried, resentful, or fearful much of the time. On our authentic path, the feelings are quite pleasant and positive. We feel hopeful, energized, motivated, empowered, confident, deeply satisfied, content, and often joyous.

Because our compass will never let us stray too far from our true path without letting us know we are off it, those living and functioning inauthentically are frequently dealing with negative emotions and experiencing discomfort, which can include health problems. People who are not on their authentic path lack energy and passion, and are not as effective in their life or work as they could be.

Almost everyone would love to eliminate the mental, emotional and/or physical pain that accompanies an unfulfilled life, but few know how to go about it. They don't realize that the place to begin is with their own perfectly functioning *internal compass* and that they can monitor it by attending to their *feelings*. They keep searching in the outer world but, since the solution isn't out there, the search continues.

If you have been searching in the outer world without success, it's time to shift your focus and the first thing to start noticing is your feelings. Know that your inner compass is flawless. Positive feelings let you know that you are on track where feelings like anxiety, frustration, anger and fear let you know that you are off track and need to make an adjustment.

If we don't pay attention to the uncomfortable feelings when they come up, our inner compass *ups the ante* and produces uncomfortable physical symptoms; insomnia, muscle tension, aches, stiff neck and shoulders, indigestion, headaches, heart palpitations and so on. People who ignore those indicators, as far too many do, often end up with a full blown illness. Then they are forced to pay attention. To understand your emotional responses, download the Emotional Guidance Scale at www.quantumleapuniversity.org/emotionalguidancescale

When the inner compass is trying to correct our path and, at the same time, conditioned beliefs keep pulling us toward what we have been taught we *should* do, the result is conflict, or feeling lost and disoriented much of the time. We feel pulled first this way and then that and no particular direction seems quite right. From this fuzzy, uncertain perspective, inner-focus seems impossible. This causes many people to shift their focus to the outer world and rely heavily on outer markers to guide their decisions and actions. The problem with relying solely on external markers is that those markers were designed by someone else and, while they might have been ideal for the person who designed them, they are only partially, and perhaps not at all, suitable for others.

It is very common for people to rush down a particular path prescribed by some success guru only to find that there is no real passion for that path and no interest in continuing down it. The path is then abandoned and the search for a new one begins. The result is many failed paths that eat up far too many years. Entire lifetimes can be wasted that way.

When people are internally misaligned, external actions will not produce long-term success. It doesn't matter how hard they work to achieve success either. If people are out of alignment with their true passion and purpose, they invariably lose momentum eventually, and lasting success eludes them.

No matter how much we study the "how to's" of success, and no matter how much we strive to apply the strategies, success is temporary at best if we are not on our own unique path. To get on our own path, we must have the seven essentials in place. Without them we can spend a lot of time spinning our wheels (working very hard, but not getting very far) or simply gathering information and storing it away.

Just as buildings without solid foundations can remain standing for awhile, so too can some people achieve a degree of success without the foundation of the seven essentials—but only *for awhile*. Just as a little tremor can send buildings with weak foundations tumbling down, so too can life's challenges bring down an individual who is trying to build success without first building the essential foundation.

Fortunately, all the searching, studying and information gathering people do in an attempt to become successful is not wasted once the seven essentials are in place. Once that firm foundation is established, all the information gathered over the years starts coming together into a cohesive whole that works. This is not conjecture. I have made the transition from constant struggle to considerable success myself and have helped hundreds of others do the same.

There is an optimal order for developing the seven essential qualities in that the first one provides a foundation for the second one to develop authentically and so on, each building on the one before it, forming a strong, dependable foundation. The seven essentials are presented here in the optimal order.

The 7 Essentials are:
1. Authentic Self-awareness and Expression
2. Clear Focus on a Purposeful Plan
3. Open, Expectant, Attitude and Beliefs
4. Solid, Healthy Boundaries
5. Self-confidence
6. Self-esteem
7. Effective Self-management (having the self-discipline to act responsibly and the courage to do the right thing)

As each essential is covered in greater detail in the following chapters, you will understand why the order laid out here is optimal.

The qualities can be developed to some degree in a different order, but generally the quality is limited and so is success. To reach grand goals and realize cherished dreams in every part of your life, and to sustain success, the seven essential qualities must be authentic and they develop authentically in the optimal order.

If you have spent years studying success principles and have still not achieved the level of success you desire, it's because one or more of the seven essentials is undeveloped or currently inaccessible.

You may be questioning how focusing on inner qualities will lead to success in the outer world. It seems counter-intuitive, which is why most people don't do it. Studies suggest that 95% of what prevents people from succeeding is *internally driven*. That means, if you are focusing on success in the external world, you are addressing only 5% of what drives it.

You won't find the seven essential qualities in most books on success because most focus on external actions; setting clear goals, associating with the right people, finding good mentors, laying out a specific plan and working it, learning about investing and money management, and so forth. Some cover the importance of having the right mindset, but the instruction here is usually quite general and confined to externally driven methods which could help if people worked at them persistently enough, but most people don't.

Some success programs also mention the importance of doing what you love or have passion around, which are certainly important, but there's more to it than is generally presented. As far too many have discovered after spending years pursuing what they thought was a passion only to lose interest, there's a big difference between interests (which most of us have lots of) and passion (our primary driver). We'll explore the differences later. For now, realize that passion proceeds from authentic self-awareness and is almost impossible to identify until we have that first essential in place.

It doesn't matter how many externally focused wealth building, success programs you take, how much you pay for them or how much time you spend working through them, none of them will lead to lasting success until the inner qualities are there. An external focus generally leads to frustration far more often than to success.

Sometimes, externally focused advice masquerades as internal. An example is the typical approach to positive thinking. After applying it for months, or even years without significant change, many people assume it is a flawed concept and throw it out. And it is flawed when it's presented as a starting point or an end in itself. The often repeated advice to think positive thoughts sounds good, but is unsound because it's impossible to maintain genuinely positive thoughts and attitudes when we are struggling to succeed. Any positive thoughts we conjure up under those circumstances feel inauthentic because they are.

Authentically positive thoughts and feelings are a result of *knowing* who you are and where you are headed in life, and of believing without a doubt that you will arrive. Genuinely positive thoughts, the kind your subconscious mind buys into and acts upon, don't occur in the face of doubt.

Another common bit of advice is to "fake it, till you make it." Fake what? Confidence? When people try, it comes across as insincere bravado or arrogance and can actually backfire. If you don't know who you are and where you want to go in life, you can't just fake the actions and attitude that will get you there. Like genuinely positive thoughts and feelings, authentic confidence cannot be faked.

We can fool a lot of people, but we cannot fool *ourselves,* at least not for long. Few people can fool themselves into believing they are happy or successful when there is ample evidence to the contrary. We either *know* who we are, where we are headed, and how to get there, or we don't. We are either doing what we love or we aren't. We either believe in our ability to reach a summit and think we're worth the effort or we don't.

And, if we *don't,* all the prompting, all the affirmations, all the advice from all the experts in the world, and all the faking won't do anything but make us feel more inauthentic, more insecure about ourselves, and more uncertain of our ability to succeed. The advice typically presented for creating success is useful for achieving success to be sure, but the odds of any of the suggested steps being put into actual practice or sustained long enough to result in real success are almost nonexistent unless the seven essential qualities are in place.

If we did all the things we are capable of doing, we would literally astound ourselves.
~Thomas Alva Edison~

CHAPTER THREE
Essential Number One
Authentic Self-Awareness & Expression

Successful people always point to passion and purpose as factors that are critical to success. As a result, almost every book on success mentions the importance of determining your true purpose and finding your passion as a prerequisite to experiencing true and lasting success.

The problem is, this prerequisite can never be met by people who don't know themselves authentically because true purpose and passion can be found in just one place; at the core of our authentic being. To get to our own true purpose and passion, we must first eliminate a lot of old baggage (programs that no longer have any value, limiting thoughts and false beliefs) which we started accumulating as children and have continued to collect throughout life.

To eliminate the old baggage and free our self to discover who we really are and what we are capable of being, we must be able to distinguish our authentic self from the many personas we adopt, and from the false mask so many of us wear.

Few people seeking success give self-awareness much thought because they assume they already have a sufficient amount of it, or that it isn't necessary to achieve success. Most people think they know themselves pretty well. After all we live with ourselves twenty-four hours a day, seven days a week. We are privy to all our thoughts and feelings, we know what we look like naked and in the finest clothes. We even know secret things about ourselves no one else knows. Surely, we know all we need to know, right?

Remember, the study I mentioned earlier which suggests that 84% of the people are not self-aware enough to report accurately on an assessment? Most of them think they know who they are. And those are just the ones who don't know their core nature. There is a much larger percentage of people (97.2%) who haven't developed their attributes to their highest potential. It seems safe to assume that, if they knew the attributes existed and that they could be far more effective if they developed them, a large percentage of people would do that.

The reason most people are not aware of their authentic self or the many beneficial attributes they were born with is because conditioning begins so early in life and continues to impact us in ways few recognize.

Most people are so thoroughly conditioned as children that by the time they reach adulthood, all they are able to see is the conditioned mask they put on as a child. The "mask" is a façade made up of beliefs and behaviors we adopted to be valued and accepted by people who were significant to us in some way.

While the mask may or may not have served our needs as children, it almost *never* serves us very well as adults. Those who believe the mask is their true self and make life decisions based on that false view, often set themselves up for a lifetime of struggle and disappointments.

Trying to function in alignment with a false mask is like swimming against the current in a swift river. No matter how strong a "swimmer" an individual may be or how hard they try, if they are swimming *against the current*, they will end each day exhausted and feeling they have made very little progress. In most cases, they *have* made very little progress because the opposing current has prevented it. When we are living life that way, we are always struggling to keep up with the demands of the day, always striving to achieve a goal or realize a dream, but never quite getting there.

We can fight our nature, but we can never win that battle. To win, we must work *with*, rather than against it. Working with nature is like floating gently down a river, just flowing along effortlessly with the current assisting us. We don't have to be strong "swimmers" to get somewhere when nature's current is assisting us along the way.

To the degree that we have been conditioned away from our nature, life is difficult. To the degree that we are working with our nature, life is satisfying and enjoyable. A life of swimming against the current is exhausting and only minimally productive, where flowing with nature allows us to easily accomplish our goals and have energy left over.

Accomplishing goals with greater ease is just one reason why discovering our authentic self is so vital. Another reason is that our true purpose and passion always emerges from our core being.

We can't have true and lasting success without purpose and passion to sustain us and keep us moving forward when things get difficult. It's what energizes, motivates and excites us. It's what lets us put in a lot of time and get a lot accomplished without the effort ever feeling like work. Passion and purpose turn work into play and make what we do so enjoyable that we just can't get enough of it. That's the stuff success is made of.

Nature provides each and every one of us with a set of attributes and abilities that allow us to be highly productive, effective and joyous when the work we do is aligned with our nature. People who accomplish amazing feats and reach astounding goals almost effortlessly are always working in concert with their nature. I have seen people take seemingly miraculous leaps forward just as a result of discovering their true nature and beginning to function from an authentic place.

Victor Frankl, in his classic book *Man's Search for Meaning* (1946) advises, "Don't aim at success—the more you aim at it and make it a target, the more you are going to miss it." He should know. He succeeded at surviving the horrible conditions of the Nazi concentration camps when thousands around him were dying. He managed to navigate through suffering by staying focused on the right things. Frankl came to realize that "the right things"—the things that guarantee success—are not "out there" somewhere. They are inside you, and when you are able to tap into that inner power, external conditions might knock you down, but they can never defeat you.

Not everyone needs such extreme conditions to get to that truth, but most people do need a catalyst of some kind to begin the search and that catalyst must lead them inward so they are searching in the right places. In an outer focused world it's easy to fall into the trap of looking outward and relying on others for validation. Know that your greatest treasures lie inside you and, when you know where to look, you *will* find them and you will love what you find. Everyone does. I've been helping people discover their authentic self for over thirty years and I have never seen a single exception.

Success is often presented as the acquisition of something—money, fancy houses, cars and other belongings, a high powered career, travel, lots of leisure time, social acuity, and so on. And certainly these can be part of the success experience, but these are the external rewards; score keepers; the *result* of doing the right things.

In the game of life, as in sports, the scores continually change, and those who are externally focused tend to worry about the scoreboard far too much. Every new variable and each new competitor becomes cause for concern because each one opens the door to potential loss.

That is *not* true of those focused on *internal success factors*. They know that once the internal factors are in place, no one can take them away. Great competitors don't bring up fears of potential defeat to self-actualized people. They present an opportunity to learn something; to hone their skills, to acquire greater strength or greater awareness.

Internally directed people know they don't lose anything to good competitors. They see good competitors as opportunities to learn and grow. With a good, solid, unchangeable core, external changes and challenges are manageable. In fact, the more a good, solid, healthy core is externally challenged, the stronger and more effective it becomes.

On the other hand, we can never be completely confident of an external position. That's why, as Frankl observed, the more you aim at success and make it your target, the more you will miss it if the external score is how you measure success.

In the stream of life, you need to know where the goal line is and you need to know how to swim—or at least stay afloat. If you are moving against the current, you need to be a very strong swimmer indeed just to stay in place. If you aren't, you are going to keep losing ground and life is going to be a frustrating experience; one in which hard work and struggle do not translate to lasting success.

If you know the nature of the stream, that is, what makes life flow for *you*, and you have found an effective way to flow *with* the current, progress will be swift and easy. That's the advantage authentic self-awareness provides. If you do nothing else, be sure you have this.

The second part of the first essential is authentic self-expression. Where self-awareness provides inner direction, self-expression allows us to connect with others in genuine ways and build strong, healthy relationships. No real measure of success has ever been gained without the help of others, and other people are far more willing to help those who they perceive as genuine.

Think about the phonies you have met; those who put on a show of bravado and act as though they are more important than other people. Are you very inclined to help them? Most of us aren't. Typically they get help only from other inauthentic people heading down the same pretentious path or those operating under fear.

Some of these people look successful on the surface, but it is always a façade. They may look like unruffled swans on the surface, but underneath they are paddling like crazy trying to keep up appearances. They live in fear that they will lose what they have gained and spend so much time trying to get more so they look better that their personal life and relationships suffer. There is no joy in that, and where joy is lacking, burnout and even serious health issues are not far behind.

The ability to connect with others authentically and to be discerning about those with whom we connect is critical to success. To build deep, meaningful relationships, we must stay authentic and associate with others who are authentic as well. Meaningful and lasting relationships rarely, if ever, occur where honesty and authenticity are lacking. Obviously, we cannot express ourselves authentically if we don't know who we are authentically. Personal success and success with others depend on it, which is why self-awareness is the *core* essential.

In my work as a psychologist, consultant, coach and trainer, everything centers around authenticity because I have found time and time again that without this core essential, nothing else works as well as it might, everything takes longer than it should, and personal satisfaction is always limited.

One client, a coach who helps women transition through life, told me that prior to discovering her true self, life on a scale of 1 to 10 was about a 7. She said she knew the concept of flow and even taught it to her clients, but had never really experienced it herself. It was in discovering her true self and beginning to express from there, she told me, that she actually experienced flow and life at the level of 10. It's a theme I have heard literally thousands of times from my clients, the coaches I train, and from their delighted clients.

Authentic self-awareness is vitally important because, until we have gained it, the other six essentials don't develop fully and are not sustainable. People waste a lot of time and money running down paths that are wrong for them, doing the wrong things and getting the wrong results because they have no idea what their authentic path looks like. Some don't even suspect they have one, so any path will do.

It's important to understand that learned skills do not define you. All normally functioning people can do anything they put their mind to, but we don't enjoy everything we are capable of doing. Some tasks are difficult to perform long-term. They frustrate us, drain us of energy and produce stress. There is a degree of resistance around such tasks even when we have learned to do them well.

My first career was in accounting and, while I knew how to do the job and was good at performing the required tasks, the work left me feeling drained and stressed. I lasted for almost eight years in that profession, but each year was more stressful than the year before. When I finally reached the point that I just couldn't face another day of endless details, I decided it was time to find another way to earn a living.

I found my authentic self and my passion through psychology, but not just any psychology. I discovered very quickly that clinical psychology was of no interest to me. I had no desire to work with pathological people. I wanted to help normal people get great results and found that I loved the psychology of motivation and performance, and loved researching factors that improved the human condition. This led to the development and delivery of many top rated workshops and to the creation of a whole host of tools that quickly transform people's lives—something I never get tired of. There is a lot of work involved in research, product development and delivering programs to groups, but I can do it for hours and hours and it never feels like work.

That's the value of tasks that are complementary to the true self. They actually energize us. We can continue to perform such tasks all day long and still have energy to spare. It is this factor that allows successful people to keep tirelessly driving toward success and loving every minute of it. Without passion for what we are doing and genuine enjoyment of the process, even if we are getting a lot done, we aren't really succeeding.

An important component of success is the deep and abiding satisfaction that only comes when we are passionately involved in what we are doing. And that is *not* something you can fake. It has to be authentic.

Because we are capable of doing anything we set our minds to, it is very common for people to choose a career path and even a life path based on external indicators as I did when I chose accounting. Some people get lucky and find a path they are passionate about before they consciously know what their passion is, but that is not the case for the majority. Most people are neither truly happy with their lives nor fully engaged in their work. According to Gallup polls conducted each year since 1996, more than 70% of people are disengaged from their work to some extent. In some instances, it's because they are in the wrong environment, but usually it's because they are in the wrong job.

Most people are aware of the resistance felt around non-preferred traits, but don't know why they feel that way or what to do about it. The subconscious mind knows what to do about it though. It simply causes the brain to disengage. It's an energy conservation strategy similar to the survival strategy. In the survival strategy, when a threat is perceived, the thinking brain shuts down, the reactive brain takes over and we go into fight, flight or freeze mode. Non-preferred tasks are not perceived as a threat, but doing them causes the brain to work harder which uses up energy, which the brain takes from the body. The subconscious mind, which regulates bodily functions then tries to restore energy to the body by distracting the brain from the energy-draining task. The result is disengagement and it happens even when we are consciously trying to prevent it.

My least preferred behavior is meticulously attending to details; checking and re-checking every little thing. The part of my brain that attends to those functions is the part that, by nature, I least prefer to use so I tend to resist those activities as much as possible. When I have to attend to details, I feel drained if I continue to do them for very long and, until I can restore my energy, I am less effective at doing more preferred activities such as researching, writing, teaching and interacting with people.

This energy/effort effect exists in everyone. We are all hard-wired to resist our least preferred tasks and to gravitate toward the most preferred. Few people are consciously aware of the energy shifts, but they should be. They provide great clues to the authentic self.

When we spend most of our time doing things that are congruent with our nature, our energy levels remain high which allows us to be more effective across the board. We are even better at handling the things we least enjoy because we have more energy to bring to the task.

Take for example, an individual whose most preferred function is actively connecting with people and experiencing life in a hands-on, bold, adventurous way. This person would have all kinds of energy, motivation and enthusiasm when doing those kinds of things. But if they had a job that required them to attend to details closely for much of the day in isolation, their energy would be so drained that by the time they left work, that they would be too exhausted to enjoy connecting with people or do anything adventurous.

Conversely, if their work allowed them to use the most preferred functions all day, in this case interacting with people in fun and adventurous ways (being an adventure tour guide for example), the individual would have more energy for other things as well. They would even be better at handling details when necessary because their higher energy would provide the fuel for the task.

The opposite would be true for someone whose most preferred function was attending to details and their least preferred was actively connecting with people. In that case, dealing with people all day long would be the drainer and attending to details, making sure everything was done right, would be the energizer.

The graph below demonstrates the energy/effort concept and how nature provides lots of energy and natural motivation for the most preferred traits (dominant and secondary) and very little for the least preferred (backup and dormant).

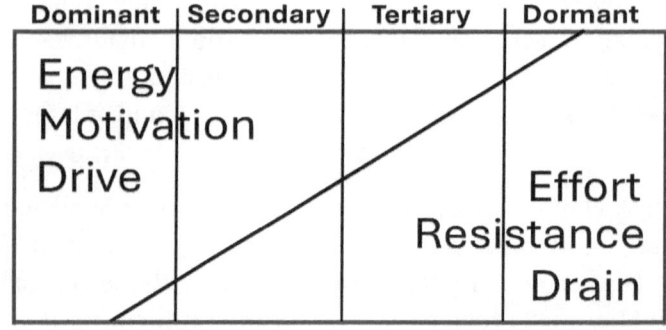

Since all normally functioning people have the capacity to use every part of their brain, we can develop skills around just about anything, but we only have so much energy to give. If we are giving it to actions that drain us, a lot of energy is being wasted and we are missing out on things that could lead to satisfaction and success.

To avoid living life at half our capacity, it is essential that we become fully aware of our authentic self so we can design our life around traits that energize and motivate us.

If you reached adulthood without knowing who you are authentically, don't count on the people who know you to be able to give you that information. Other people see only what we show them, and often, when we have been strongly conditioned away from our authentic self, what we show them is the *mask* we put on as a child. Even when others see us differently than we see ourselves, we are often skeptical of their appraisal.

Don't count on most assessments either, because most assessments are designed to expand on your current knowledge of yourself. They measure and report self-perception, observable traits or preferred functions. The problem is, if your awareness is of your conditioned mask rather than of your authentic self, it is the conditioned mask that you will report and which typical assessments will reflect back to you, which simply deepens your conviction that the false self is real.

Every truly successful person you will ever encounter, without exception, is living and working in ways that are congruent with their natural passions. If you aren't already certain that you know who you are authentically and are expressing it through your true passion, discovering your true nature is the first thing you need to focus on.

If you have had the experience of setting out on a path that seemed right and giving it your all, only to find that you lost momentum and couldn't sustain the pace, know that it has nothing to do with your ability to succeed.

Like a swimmer swimming against a strong current, it's impossible to keep up the pace and go as far as we actually have the capacity to go when we are working against our nature. To know what we are capable of, we need to be traveling a complementary path and to do that we have to know our true nature.

If you are not happy and content with who you are – not necessarily *where* you are in life, but how you perceive yourself – you can bet that you don't yet know your authentic self fully. I make that statement without the slightest reservation because I have found time and time again that people are infinitely happier and far more effective when functioning from their true nature. They are better at managing their life and outcomes than most people too because they have a solid sense of self that keeps them moving in the right direction easily and at a satisfying pace, no matter what is going on around them.

While there are many things you can do to increase self-awareness, I only know of one tool that can get past the conditioned mask and to the authentic self quickly and effectively, the *CORE Multidimensional Awareness Profile* (CORE MAP). CORE MAP is an in-depth assessment which provides measures from multiple angles; how you see yourself, how you show up in the world, what you have developed, how effectively you are using your natural traits, strengths and energizers, and more. This is one of the tools my company trains coaches to facilitate and, in trained hands, I know of nothing that works better or faster. CORE MAP exists for three reasons:

1. I spent the first 32 years of my life lost and struggling, and I know how limiting and painful that can be. I wanted a way to help others avoid that path, or get off of it as quickly as possible, so I set out to find one.

2. Years of researching successful people made it clear that authentic self-awareness was the foundation of every true success, which made it clear that not having that vital piece in place could result in many years of unnecessary struggle as it had for me.

3. After many years of searching and researching hundreds of assessments and personal development programs, I was not able to find one that got past the programming and false perceptions, so working with a team of brilliant developers, we developed one - CORE MAP.

That was in 1996. Since then we have administered tens of thousands of assessments, and trained and certified hundreds of coaches around the globe to administer and facilitate this powerfully accurate and predictive assessment. Thousands of lives and relationships have been transformed as a result, as have many leaders, teams, and even entire organizations.

CORE MAP is a facilitated assessment because no computer generated cookie-cutter report can help people get past conditioning that has kept them blind to their truth or stuck far below their natural potential. And no computer generated report provides the guidance necessary for helping people develop to their highest potential. In fact, when people identify with a false mask, all most assessments do is deepen the conviction that the false self is real, which leaves people stuck in an ineffective and unsatisfying cycle.

I have provided a free tool, the *CORE Energy Evaluator*, which you can access at www.quantumleapuniversity.org/energyeval. It will help you discover the attributes you have the most and least energy around. Knowing what energizes you, and what you feel resistance to, is a great first step in knowing your true nature. Our brains are hard-wired to perform specific tasks easily, and when we are performing those tasks, or even imagine ourselves performing them, we feel energized and enthusiastic. On the other hand, we feel resistance and lower energy around the tasks we least prefer. The *CORE Energy Evaluator* doesn't give you the whole picture like CORE MAP does, but it's a good first step, and all some people need to get headed in the right direction.

If, after completing the *CORE Energy Evaluator*, you are still not sure, or if you want a more complete map so you know exactly what to focus on to develop yourself to your highest potential in the fastest way possible, consider taking CORE MAP. Many people have reported that it was one of the best investments they ever made.

However you choose to achieve this goal, realize that you *must* have a clear sense of your authentic self before you can create a clear vision of where you are headed (the next essential step). Self-awareness is the foundation for everything else. Your first task then is to **discover your authentic self**. Once you do, you will be amazed at how quickly and easily your capacity to accomplish your goals develops.

If you would like to learn more about CORE MAP, go to https://coremap.com

To take CORE MAP, go to www.quantumleapuniversity.org and contact one of the CORE certified coaches you will find listed under "Find a Coach." The coaches listed there are highly trained and very effective. They can generally get you farther in a few hours than most other methods can get in months or even years.

Authentic Self-Expression

Before moving on to essential number two (clear purpose and focus), I want to make you aware of a trap that derails a lot of people so you can avoid it. I call it a *proficiency trap*.

We have already covered the fact that we can do just about anything we decide to do. That's because every trait available to any normally functioning person is available to all other normally functioning people to some extent. But not all of the things we are capable of doing are enjoyable or energizing and, when they aren't, they drain our energy and greatly slow our progress.

The things we are capable of doing, whether natural or learned, can be considered strengths in that they help us accomplish something. But strengths and energizers are two different things. Strengths aid us in getting specific things done. Energizers motivate, inspire and drive us forward and allow us to get a lot accomplished almost effortlessly and without resistance or energy drain.

The trap we get caught in is assuming that because we are good at something, it must be a natural attribute. The reality is, we can become proficient at a lot of things if we practice enough. I'm good with numbers, for example, and have training in accounting, but I don't enjoy accounting. I resist work that requires attending to details too closely and I'm soon drained by that type of work. But, because I am capable of doing the work well, I got a lot of positive feedback from others when I was working in that field, which kept me in that role a lot longer than I wanted to be. That is how we get caught in a proficiency trap. We keep doing work that drains our energy and limits our successes because we know how to do it and get positive feedback from others, or because that's the only way we know to earn a living.

The exceptional performance we often call genius occurs when the skills we learn enhance our natural traits rather than compete with them. That rarely happens because we live in an externally focused world that seldom considers natural traits as an important first factor in choosing the education and training we get. That's why so many people are working at jobs they don't especially like and feeling tired and uninspired.

Drained of energy and enthusiasm, the masses continue to drag themselves through life, doing what they must to meet expectations, and searching the external world for something to boost their energy and make life more interesting. Energy drinks have become a $50 billion industry and entertainment, the method of choice for adding a little interest to life, topped $2 trillion in 2015.

You don't find genuinely successful people downing caffeine-laced energy drinks or spending a lot of time distracting themselves. They are too excited about their own lives to waste time watching other people playing games or acting out parts that mimic life. They don't want or need meaningless distractions because life is just too much fun.

Living authentically and in harmony with natural strengths makes the actions successful people take feel effortless. They look effortless too which is why people are so awed by how easy and effortless the lives of successful people seem, and at the huge amounts of energy, enthusiasm, motivation, drive and confidence they seem to have. People who are still striving to succeed often try to get the trappings first thinking they will have the energy, enthusiasm, motivation, drive and confidence once they have the money and freedom they seek. That's backwards and it never works.

Another thing that limits success for people is the habit of putting their self last in life. This is especially common when an individual is stressed or overworked. Most of us grew up being told that we should put others first and that anything else was selfish. It's a very common theme in religion, in many homes, and even in the business world. Those who have bought into this message generally make sure every project gets done, everything is right, and everyone is happy before considering or attending to their own needs. The problem is that there never comes a time when everything is done, everything is right and everyone is happy. So those who hold this belief never get around to attending to self on any significant level. The eventual result is burnout, frustration, suppressed anger, anxiety, depression, joylessness, and the illnesses negative emotions foster.

As you take inventory of yourself, check to make sure you are not caught in a proficiency trap, doing work you are good at, but don't enjoy, and be sure you are not putting your own needs last. If you are, please understand that you are doing yourself and those you care about a great disservice. We can only give to others what we own, and if you are running on empty most of the time, what you likely own is frustration, impatience, anger, anxiety, depression, and the disappointment that comes from constant struggling to make progress; not exactly good things to be sharing.

As you are in the midst of creating a successful life, deferring time for yourself may seem like a good idea. It isn't. Don't do it. You will achieve success a lot faster if you give yourself the gift of time spent doing things you enjoy. Make it a habit to monitor your feelings and take a break when you are feeling stressed. Just ten to fifteen minutes of doing something you find fun or relaxing can re-energize you and clear your head which will make you far more effective. Not only will you get more done, you'll be happier, a lot more pleasant to be around, and ultimately a lot more successful.

Journaling is another highly effective way to monitor and manage your responses and life outcomes. Choose a journal that speaks to you. Download the file with journal prompts for developing each essential at www.quantumleapuniversity.org/journalprompts

Every great artist was first an amateur.
~Ralph Waldo Emerson~

CHAPTER FOUR
Essential Number Two
Clear Purpose & Focus

Once you are clear about who you are authentically and what you are passionate about, you are ready to begin laying out your plan for getting from where you are now to where you want to go. This is a process of clarifying your purpose and defining your life path.

Many people try to begin their journey to success here, but without authentic self-awareness, they often find themselves running down many paths that lead nowhere. I know from first-hand experience and from helping thousands of people get redirected over the years, that trying to lay out a plan without authentic self-awareness, is a long and largely fruitless journey, mostly because it's spent just groping in the dark. People who don't know who they are usually don't know what they want either. And, unless we know what we want, the likelihood of laying out a plan that actually works is almost nonexistent.

A solid sense of self is the compass that keeps us from losing our way. It's the guiding principle that informs our decisions and points us toward what's really important. If we don't know what's important to us, success is often approached as simply a means of making more money and, when that's the primary goal, we become susceptible to anyone with a seemingly viable idea. Any scheme that has the potential to generate money gets considered and all too often, acted upon, which can keep people running down the dead end avenues for years, even for a lifetime. People do sometimes chance onto the right path that way, but the odds are so small that I sure wouldn't want to gamble my life and happiness on it.

The journey to any worthwhile goal will present us with challenges and, unless we are genuinely passionate about the journey we are on, the challenges that inevitably come up can cause us to get discouraged and abandon the path before we achieve success.

I have been in business since 1984 and have faced many challenges that, at times, seemed insurmountable. Had I not been very clear about who I am and what my mission and purpose are, I most certainly would have given up. And, had I given up, I would still be living the life of quiet desperation I once knew. But giving up isn't the biggest problem. The biggest problem is never getting started.

Without the drive born of passion, few people will take the time or make the effort to lay out an actual plan for achieving their goals and realizing their dream. Even those who are tenacious enough to hang in there long enough to develop goals and create plans generally will not stick with them once challenges arise if they lack true passion for what they are doing. Challenges have a way of eroding enthusiasm and once enthusiasm goes, interest in continuing along a challenging path quickly dies making the outcome no longer worth the effort. The typical response once interest wanes, is to abandon the endeavor and go looking for another opportunity.

If this has happened to you before, or even several times before, it does *not* mean there is anything wrong with you. It only means that you have not yet found your passion.

Interests Are Not the Same as Passion

Many people mistake interests for passion, but they are very different. Lots of things can get our interest. We might be interested in music, snow skiing, mystery novels, cooking, gardening and a whole host of other things. Interest alone doesn't grab hold of our heart and soul, and drive us forward. Only passion does that. Interests are generally centered around external things. Passion always emerges from within. It informs your mission and sets you on a path filled with meaning and purpose.

Undiscovered passion often shows up as a longing we can't eliminate. It's what keeps us searching and trying one thing after another. Without passion, you cannot know your purpose and, until you know your purpose, you cannot develop goals and plans you will stick with long enough to succeed.

When people try to begin with goal setting, they often come to the conclusion that goal setting doesn't work. And, without a passion-driven purpose, goal setting doesn't work very well because passionless goals have no staying power.

Two Kinds of Purpose

There are two kinds of purpose and it's important to get clear on both so you don't come to a place years down the road where you have a need to start over. The first kind of purpose is short-term. What makes it short-term is that it comes to an end when a situation changes.

An example would be a parent who is working three jobs to be sure her children get what they need. Once her children are grown and on their own, that purpose will cease to drive her. Unless she also has a personal, passion-driven purpose, she will experience what is referred to as "empty nest syndrome" and her life will feel meaningless. To avoid being unhappy, she must then begin again, searching for another purpose.

The other kind of purpose keeps life filled with meaning right up to the end. This is your core purpose. When short-term purpose is supported by a personal, passion-driven core purpose, even the short-term is more successful. With a core purpose, the mother who is working three jobs to support her children doesn't neglect to take care of her own health or to prepare for her own future. She knows that when her children are grown, she will begin an exciting, new, and well thought out adventure, and she prepares for it even as she fulfills her short-term purpose.

As you begin developing your plans and goals, be sure they are built around your core purpose. If they are, nothing will derail you. Even apparent failures will become a source of learning that will help you hone your skills and get back on track with greater confidence in your ability to meet challenges.

Be clear about any short-term purposes that now drive your behaviors. Know that they will come to an end and know where you want to be when they do. Also know who you want to be part of your journey so you can begin developing plans and goals that include them.

Say, for example, you are working for a company, but know that to fulfill your core purpose you will need to own your own business. However, you have children and know you need to keep your current job until they have completed their college education. And say you also know that you would like to have a family-owned business where any of your children who are interested can be part of it. By knowing your core purpose and planning ahead, you have the opportunity to talk with your children about the business you plan to build, which gives those who are interested the opportunity to choose a college major or life path that will enhance their contribution and increase the chance for success. By knowing where you are headed both your short-term purpose and your long-term core purpose can be enhanced.

The Failure Fallacy

As we go through life, it is inevitable that we meet with failure occasionally. People who aren't failing aren't trying anything new. They aren't stretching themselves and, if they aren't stretching, they will most definitely not experience lasting success.

Should a route you choose turn out not to be the best or wisest one to continue along, don't let the mistaken notion that to abandon that path means you failed. There are actually only five ways to fail, and abandoning a non-productive path is *not* one of them.

The five ways to fail are:

1. Dreaming of a better outcome, but never getting started. No action is a guarantee of failure.
2. Continuing down a path you know is *wrong* for you to appease others, or out of fear. Realize that your comfort zone is not a haven. It's a prison keeping you locked away from success.
3. Not taking a path you know is *right* for you because of several unsuccessful attempts or because you fear you might not succeed if you try it.
4. Letting distractions take you down an undefined path or one that has been defined by someone else.
5. Settling for less than you are capable of achieving.

If you are paying attention, your inner-compass will always discourage you from traveling too far down a path that is wrong for you. Long before you get far enough down a path to realize that it isn't the right one, your inner-compass is sending out signals of discomfort. By learning to pay attention to those signals early you can save a whole lot of time, energy and money, not to mention frustration.

All motivation occurs as a result of our efforts to move away from pain or toward pleasure. So abandoning something that is becoming more and more uncomfortable is a very natural course of action. Be thankful for those feelings of discomfort when they show up and *pay attention* to them. They are clear indicators that you are off your path.

Clearly, ceasing to follow the wrong path is superior to continuing on it. Those who continue to do the wrong thing or pursue the wrong goals, once they realize they are wrong are more than foolish—they are insane. One definition of insanity is continuing to do the same thing and expecting different results. It's even more insane to keep doing what you know to be the wrong thing and expecting a good result.

You can waste a lot of time switching from one wrong path to another, but you can waste an entire lifetime staying on the wrong path because you believe abandoning it amounts to failure. Stay aware of the five ways to fail so you don't get caught in that trap.

The only way to spend time wisely and well is to spend it *on your own path*; the one that is exactly right for you. So it is wise to take the time to discover what is authentic to you before you decide on a path to travel. Choose not to waste time groping for the right opportunity or hoping to stumble across the right path. That's a very ineffective strategy. Your life is far too valuable to subject it to blind experiments.

There are many reasons why people get and stay on the wrong path. The pursuit of money is one common one. Another is trying to meet someone else's expectations. But, probably the most common reason is not knowing self well enough to define an authentic path. When this is the case, groping through life helping someone else realize their dream is the only option.

None of us come into the world with a set of instructions, but life doesn't have to be a blind experiment. There is a tried and true formula that works every time. Most people don't know that, so they keep wandering through life with no sense of purpose and no idea where they are going.

Without a workable formula, life feels like a deep, dark forest which we are right in the middle of without a clue as to how to get out so we just keep wandering in circles, expending a great deal of effort but getting nowhere.

Without a sense of direction, we have only two choices; keep trying, or give up and resign ourselves to being lost. Studies suggest that 80% of people give up. Only 20% keep looking. Of that 20% only 3% eventually succeed.

In the forest analogy, of 100 people, 80 would just sit down and hope to get rescued while 20 would keep trying, But without a workable strategy or tools to help them, 17 of that 20 would just keep walking in circles. Only 3 would eventually devise a method, such as marking trees, to help them find a way out.

Imagine how different things would be if the people in that forest had a perfectly functioning compass and knew with certainty the direction in which they wanted to go.

In life, the compass is self-awareness which includes knowing one's self authentically and also being aware of the emotions that act as indicators to let us know whether we are on track or off. Not many people are that deeply self-aware. The few who are have an abiding sense of "True North" which acts as an ever constant center that guides decisions and keeps them tracking toward their own personal version of success.

One way to determine your authentic path without knowing your core nature is to pay close attention to your emotional responses. This method won't help you discover your authentic self, but as a guide to your authentic path, it's quite accurate. Positive emotions indicate that you are on your path and negative ones indicate that you are off. The only caution here is to avoid conjuring up false positives. You will know you are doing that if seemingly positive feelings fade quickly, or are there at times and not there at other times. Genuine feelings don't vary.

Once you are clear on your ultimate destination, you can begin laying out milestones so you can track your progress. Milestones are a little different than goals in that they are meant to measure progress rather than define an action. You will need goals too, but laying out the general direction and the milestones will make filling in the details easier. Don't let the idea of planning deter you, even if you don't like details. Once you have the path laid out in a general way, planning the steps you will take can be great fun when driven by passion.

A Word of Warning

Once you have found your passion and your purpose, rushing off in that direction without a plan can be very tempting, especially when you have been searching for a long time. Resist the temptation. Take the time to devise a plan of action so your focus remains clear.

For many years I knew what my passion was and thought I could just wing my way through life and business. I wasted a lot of years that way. I made progress, but it was slow and often grueling. In retrospect, I can see that the progress I did make always occurred in areas where the goal was clear and I had a plan, however informal, for getting there.

You may have discovered, as I did, that you can waste a *lot* of time and money chasing lovely rainbows, bright shiny objects, and half-defined dreams. To stop doing that, you need two things: self-discipline and clarity around your passion, purpose and mission. You will get where you want to go a *lot* faster with clarity and a lot easier with self-discipline.

Once I discovered and defined the seven essentials (through planned research), realized the extreme importance of taking this step, and began moving through life more purposefully, I stopped being an accidental tourist and began to make real progress, and so will you.

You don't have to have the whole journey planned out before developing the other five essential qualities, but you will need at least a sense of direction and an outline to have a genuinely open, expectant attitude and belief that you will arrive (essential number 3).

The steps you will take as you begin developing essential number four (solid personal and relationship boundaries) will give you more tools for adding detail to your journey. So get out your journal, reference the journal prompts for essential number four and lay out as much as you can for now. The details will come as you develop the other essentials and gain more clarity. Please don't neglect this essential step. It will make your progress much faster and your journey much more fun! Time to journal - www.quantumleapuniversity.org/journalprompts

*The most direct route to success is not a map.
It's your mind.*
~Sherry Buffington~

CHAPTER FIVE
Essential Number Three
Open, Expectant Attitude & Beliefs

There has been so much written about maintaining a positive attitude, thinking positive thoughts, keeping the faith, and believing in one's self and abilities that this factor almost goes without saying. It gets a lot of press in books and in films such as *The Secret*, because it is an essential factor, but here's the thing: about the only thing this factor *alone* will get you is a lot of frustration.

An open, expectant attitude and believing in positive outcomes is what motivates us to keep trying, but in and of itself, this belief can be downright dangerous. To demonstrate how, let's toss ourselves back into that dense forest for a moment.

Imagine the earlier scenario where the people there had no idea where they were or how to determine their coordinates. Now imagine that you are among them and, after taking a few paths and realizing you were hopelessly lost, you decided to sit beneath a tree and think positive thoughts. You vividly imagine being rescued and fervently believe someone will come to save you.

This could happen, of course, provided someone had a general idea of where you were and was determined to look until you were found. But, what if no one knew? What do you suppose your odds of getting out of that forest alive would be? How much better would your chances be if you started thinking creatively about surviving and then took specific, planned actions?

I hope you can see how ineffective an open, expectant, positive attitude would be without knowing where you want to go, developing a plan and having the determination to take the right actions. Yet, without the right attitude, you wouldn't keep trying. Once you met with defeat a time or two and realized you were going in circles, only the right attitude would allow you to adjust your thoughts, feelings and behaviors, and keep trying new things.

The reason many people have trouble maintaining a good attitude is because they lack faith in themselves or they believe in one or more of the failure fallacies. Lack of faith often occurs as a result of struggling against the current of life every day without knowing why, or what to do about it.

With an awareness of who we came into the world to be, where we are headed and why, we quickly become more positive about our prospects. Nature provides us with so many wonderful attributes to work with, and when we are aware of them, we discover we have a lot more tools in our tool kit than we ever imagined. Just knowing that we have untapped abilities can create a positive shift.

It's empowering to know that, although we may be off our path, we are not broken. We each came into the world *perfectly suited* to do the exact things we most desire. This is something that becomes readily apparent once we know who we are authentically and begin expressing from that space.

Though the messages we get through advertising and social networks can lead us to want the things that are presented as desirable, these are not authentic desires and they don't inspire action beyond acquisition. Authentic desires are those that fire up our mind, feed our soul and continue to fuel motivation. Their fulfillment adds meaning and purpose to life.

Many people find it hard to believe that we already have everything we need to be fulfilled and happy. For some odd reason, these skeptics find it easier to believe that they are frail and limited; that only a select few have what it takes to live a happy, fulfilled, successful life.

Granted, observing the human condition overall seems to validate that assumption, but looking at the *reason* so many people are living lives of quiet desperation and so few living full, abundant lives, it becomes obvious that the problem is not lack of capacity, but lack of awareness.

When we have been taught from the time we were small children that our worth is in making sure other people are pleased with how we show up in the world, it's easy to access our shortcomings and overlook our strengths and inherent abilities; to magnify our flaws and minimize our greatness. Doing that is like looking at a thousand piece puzzle of a truly beautiful picture which has one piece missing and being unable to appreciate the picture, or the fact that there a 999 pieces in place, because that one missing piece grabs our attention and shifts our mood to one of dissatisfaction.

No one is perfect. No one has lived a life so charmed that none of the pieces ever got lost. We are all flawed to some extent, but it's the flaws that make us unique and give us that human quality of being able to reach out to others with empathy and caring.

Successful people aren't flawless; far from it. It's just that they have discovered that flaws are part of the fabric of life and only a small part of their personal mix. They know that the larger part is powerful and dependable and worthy of the well-being all humans naturally seek. Where the masses are focused on the missing piece, the successful are focused on the pieces that are there and which present a beautiful, one-of-a-kind masterpiece.

What does your masterpiece look like? Do you know or at least have some idea? If you don't, go back to the first essential and discover it. Once you have it, I promise you, your attitude will be very positive. You will expect great things from yourself and you will believe that you can make them happen. You will know that you have everything you need to fulfill every authentic desire you have.

Once you understand that the only thing preventing you from reaching your cherished goals is conditioning—old baggage you have been carrying around for years—and once you realize you can put that baggage down (and do that) you won't need many attitude adjustments.

The state of being which Csikszentmihalyi called flow occurs occasionally for some people, but it's an almost constant state for people who are fully aware and are expressing themselves authentically. To the extent that we are living and working in harmony with our authentic self, we are in flow and are just naturally more optimistic.

In an interview, Csikszentmihalyi was asked how one would recognize an optimal experience. He replied, "By the fact that you are completely immersed in what you are doing; that your level of concentration is very high; that you know what you have to do moment by moment and are joyous in doing it; that you have immediate and precise feedback as to how well you are doing; and that you feel your abilities are stretched, but you are not overwhelmed by the opportunities before you. In other words, the challenges are perfectly balanced with your skills. When those conditions are present, you forget about the things that bother you in everyday life. You forget the self as an entity separate from what is going on. You feel you are part of something greater and you are just moving along with the flow of the activity."

This describes flow as an experience and most people can identify with it as an experience that occurs occasionally when they are immersed in something they find fascinating. Imagine being in that state most of the time. Imagine how effective you would be if your concentration level was very high most of the time; if you knew what you had to do moment by moment and were joyous in doing it; if the challenges you faced were perfectly balanced with your skills, and you were constantly aware of being part of something great. Imagine what your mood, attitude and beliefs would be from that state of being.

That's the stuff success is made of, and it's the state people who are living and functioning from their authentic core experience most of the time. Is it any wonder they get so much done with such ease?

When we are aware of our natural skills and abilities and begin purposefully developing them, we become proficient very rapidly. As we become more proficient our outcomes improve and, as outcomes improve, we become more positive, our belief in our abilities increases. We expect to succeed, and the expectant attitude further increases the ability to perform, which accelerates our successes.

Influence

The benefits of positive thoughts are mostly internal, but the positive attitude they inspire directly impacts our ability to connect with and influence other people. No one achieves success independently. All true and lasting success comes through the help and cooperation of others.

Every success is interdependent and synchronistic so the better we are at inspiring and influencing others, the more likely we are to succeed.

Positive thinking has been taken too far in some circles. So much so that there are people who insist positive thoughts, beliefs and expectations are all that are necessary for success. Don't believe it! As important an element as this is, it is only *one element*. Don't let all the hoopla around this aspect of success cause you to depend on it more than you should, but don't discount its importance either. Neither response will serve you well.

Positive thoughts, beliefs, and intent keep us going when times get tough. They provide us with the impetus to pick ourselves up and get back in the game. They get us past the jagged rocks and steep slopes as we climb to the top of our own special mountain. And they are essential to the development of the next three qualities for success.

Time to journal - www.quantumleapuniversity.org/journalprompts

*To reach any summit,
we must first believe we can.*

~Sherry Buffington~

> *If civilization is to survive, we must cultivate the science of relationships; the ability of all peoples, of all kinds, to live together in the same world at peace.*
>
> ~Franklin D. Roosevelt~

CHAPTER SIX
Essential Number Four
Solid Personal & Relationship Boundaries

When you add open, expectant, positive attitudes and beliefs to a clear sense of direction and a plan for arriving at your intended destination, you begin to feel quite confident *provided* you have built healthy enough boundaries to prevent others from pushing you around or pulling you off your chosen course.

Developing healthy boundaries is the fourth essential factor and the subject of this chapter. Healthy boundaries need to be developed from both the inside and the outside.

On the inside, (personal boundaries) we need to know who we are and who we are not so the opinions of others don't cause us to question our concept of self.

On the outside, (relationship boundaries) we need to know what we will and will not accept from others and from ourselves. It is important to have both the in and out sides of our boundaries defined and fortified.

Healthy boundaries are solid and not easily distorted. When they are weak, squishy or worse, non-existent, others can impose their wills, opinions and agendas on us too easily and pull us off course. Without good solid boundaries we tend to get so busy trying to please others, or avoid their disapproval, that we have little time to even think about, much less pursue, our own goals and dreams. Boundaries that are too easily shifted or invaded by others are not solid enough to allow us to build a firm personal foundation or effectively manage our relationships, and both are essential to long-term success.

Healthy boundaries are not rigid either. They are malleable enough to evolve and grow as we grow, but firm enough that *we* are the ones determining the scope and direction of the evolution, not someone else.

It is not possible to build solid, healthy boundaries until we know who we are authentically. And it's difficult to honor and protect our authenticity without solid boundaries, which is why both are essential.

Until we know who we are authentically and what we want, we can't separate our own wants and needs from those of others and, until we can do that, we can't know if the path we choose is our own authentic path or one that was imposed by others. We can't know if the choices we make will move us forward or hold us back. More often than not, the agendas of others are designed to advance *their* dreams, not ours. So it is highly likely that we are being held back if other people are determining our lives for us.

Solid boundaries are also not possible without positive beliefs and expectations. If we didn't believe we could succeed at creating and sustaining healthy boundaries and expect a good outcome from having built them, we wouldn't even try.

This is where it seems to get sticky. Without boundaries, other people's agenda's continually push us off course and undermine our own intentions. We have no clear sense of direction, and often no clear sense of self. Without a sense of direction or self, we cease to believe that we can succeed. But, we have to believe that we can succeed to begin building healthy personal boundaries.

This vicious loop begins early in life when others are calling the shots. We don't have the skills or knowledge to determine our own life and outcomes when we are children and, by the time we reach the point in life where we do have them; the unhealthy pattern has already been established.

Few people have the benefit of parents and teachers who taught them to respect their own space. Few learned how to effectively assert their rights either and, without assertiveness skills, we have only two choices when things are less than ideal. We can comply with the demands and expectations of others, or we can rebel. If we comply, we lose our sense of self. If we rebel, we create conflict. Most people are conflict avoidant so choose the path of compliance, which is why so many people reach adulthood without a clear sense of who they are.

Once we get caught in the vicious loop, it's hard to imagine how we can get out of it. If we need to believe that we can succeed before we can build solid boundaries, but we need solid boundaries before we can succeed, where does one begin?

Obviously, you can't begin with solid boundaries. That's why it's essential number four. You need a solid sense of self before you can begin working on developing healthy boundaries, but you want to start building boundaries as soon as you have authentic self-awareness. Establishing boundaries quickly will strengthen your sense of self and protect you from those who think they know how you should live your life better than you do.

To build healthy personal boundaries it is important to know which of the attributes you identify with are authentic to you and which you bought from others. Until you can separate the two and decide which are really yours and which you should let go of, all the messages and misperceptions gathered over the years will continue to falsely define you.

Good, solid boundaries provide a means for establishing your worth and purposefully directing your own life. Everyone needs them and the better defined they are, the better your life and outcomes will be.

There are exercises at the end of this chapter to help you begin building good solid boundaries and you will want to get started, but it's important to know that this is not something you will complete all at once. It's an evolving process which you can and should continue to build upon as you become more and more aware of your true wants and needs, and of what you are willing to accept into your life and experiences and what you will no longer tolerate.

Your first task in this area is to build the internal *personal* boundaries: who you are and are not. Once that is done, you can more easily build and maintain external *relationship* boundaries.

Healthy relationship boundaries require that you know what you are and are not willing to accept from yourself and from others. *Self* is included in relationship boundaries as well as personal boundaries because our relationship with self is just as important as our relationships with others. To have integrity, we need to know what we are and are not willing to accept from ourselves and keep those boundaries as firm as the ones we set for others.

To have good solid boundaries you must be able to define and articulate four things:

1. Who you ARE
2. Who you are NOT
3. What you WILL accept from self or others
4. What you will NOT accept from self or others

Exercise for Creating Boundaries

To begin establishing personal and relationship boundaries, you will need two charts: one to define personal attributes and the other to define acceptable behaviors and relationship dynamics.

The subconscious mind, which pretty much runs the show, communicates in pictures and feelings, not in words. It takes words that have meaning, however, and translates that meaning into pictures and feelings that it can process. The charts you will create provide a visual boundary which separate the attributes and actions you want to own from the ones you choose to disown. What the subconscious mind does with this is fascinating. I have done these charts for myself and have helped many others with theirs and the results for almost everyone are quite remarkable.

In my case, when I first created my charts, on the relationship chart, one of the things I put in the "I will NOT accept" space was "being manipulated." At the time, I had no skills for preventing myself from being manipulated and didn't even recognize some forms of manipulation for what they were. I was pretty passive when it came to dealing with other people at the time and people regularly took advantage of that fact.

Within weeks of declaring that I would not accept being manipulated, I developed an intense desire to learn more about manipulation and how to avoid it. Ultimately, I learned so much about it, and was so successful in eliminating it from my life that I developed an assertiveness workshop to help others do the same and thousands of people have benefitted from it.

The only thing I could attribute the sudden urge to learn to be more assertive to at the time was the chart, but I couldn't imagine it could be that easy. In the years since, having taught this method to many other people and gotten their feedback, and having studied the way the subconscious mind works, I now know for certain that the catalyst was working with those charts. So, even if you are feeling a little skeptical, start defining your personal boundaries using this system and see what happens.

The charts are very simple to create—not so simple to populate for some people, but well worth the effort. The reason many people have trouble populating the charts in the beginning is because they aren't clear on which attributes they own and which they don't own, or they feel uncomfortable claiming really positive traits, such as brilliant, influential, powerful, etc. The key is, if you want to own an attribute, claim it. If there is something you currently identify with which you don't like and don't want to keep, disown it. It helps to consult your inner compass as you decide what to keep and what to discard.

To Create Your Boundaries Charts

1. Download Boundary Charts at www.quantumleapuniversity.org/boundarycharts or you can use a poster board if you prefer a larger model (examples on page 59). If creating your own, draw a circle that takes up about half of the area. Use a plate, saucer or other circular object to make it, or create it on your computer. If the circle is misshapen, it will become a distraction. On one sheet write **"I Am"** on the inside of the circle and **"I Am NOT"** on the outside of the circle.

2. Using the first "I AM/Am NOT" sheet, put all the things you do *not* want to claim *outside* the circle and all the things you *do* want inside it. The visual barrier created between the attributes inside the circle and those outside allows the subconscious mind to organize the attributes into themes and then build a picture around the themes. It takes ownership of the attributes inside the circle and disowns those on the outside.

   List everything you know, believe or have been told about yourself. This is the not-so-simple part. It requires some real thought. *Only positive, beneficial attributes go inside* the circle because that is all you ultimately want to claim. All the negative, limiting, non-beneficial things go *outside* the circle.

3. Decide which attributes and way of living and interacting would make you really proud to be who you are. Only these go *inside* the circle. All the things that you dislike in yourself; that you wish you didn't do, and all the things you are unwilling to accept from yourself or others go on the outside.

4. On the second sheet, write "**I Will Accept**" inside the circle and "**I Will NOT Accept**" on the outside. This circle defines your relationship boundaries, including your relationship with yourself.

5. On the *inside*, put all the things you love and enjoy about your relationship with yourself and your relationships with others. On the *outside* list all the things you just tolerate or that irritate, anger, or worry you.

6. Decide what you are *no longer* willing to allow or tolerate from others and list them. Even if you don't know how to effect a particular change right now put it out there.

7. Put your two charts somewhere where you will see them regularly. When you stop noticing them, move them to a new location and keep doing that until you have a clear picture of what is inside and outside of both circles. The more novel the placement, the better. The mind tends to notice things that are novel and ignore things that have been around awhile. For example, you ignore the calendar on your desk or wall until you need to refer to it. The same occurs with furniture or anything else we leave in the same place. So move your boundaries list around and keep adding to it until you know without a doubt who you really are and what you will accept into your life. You will love the result of being clear on who you are and are not, and what you will and will not accept into your life.

Essential Number Four Solid Personal & Relationship Boundaries

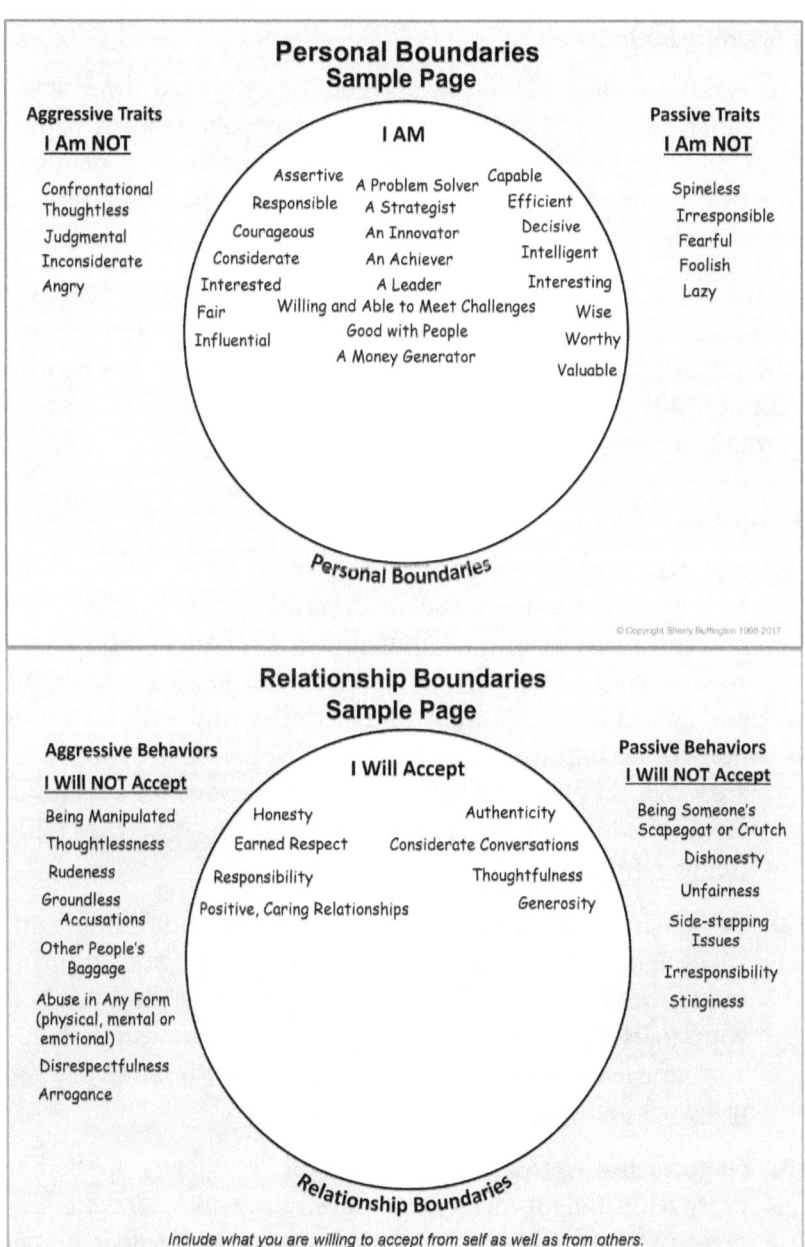

Personal Boundaries
Sample Page

Aggressive Traits
I Am NOT

Confrontational
Thoughtless
Judgmental
Inconsiderate
Angry

I AM

Assertive
Responsible
Courageous
Considerate
Interested
Fair
Influential
A Problem Solver
A Strategist
An Innovator
An Achiever
A Leader
Willing and Able to Meet Challenges
Good with People
A Money Generator
Capable
Efficient
Decisive
Intelligent
Interesting
Wise
Worthy
Valuable

Passive Traits
I Am NOT

Spineless
Irresponsible
Fearful
Foolish
Lazy

Personal Boundaries

© Copyright Sherry Buffington 1998-2017

Relationship Boundaries
Sample Page

Aggressive Behaviors
I Will NOT Accept

Being Manipulated
Thoughtlessness
Rudeness
Groundless Accusations
Other People's Baggage
Abuse in Any Form (physical, mental or emotional)
Disrespectfulness
Arrogance

I Will Accept

Honesty
Earned Respect
Responsibility
Positive, Caring Relationships
Authenticity
Considerate Conversations
Thoughtfulness
Generosity

Passive Behaviors
I Will NOT Accept

Being Someone's Scapegoat or Crutch
Dishonesty
Unfairness
Side-stepping Issues
Irresponsibility
Stinginess

Relationship Boundaries

Include what you are willing to accept from self as well as from others.

© Copyright Sherry Buffington 1998-2017

Maintaining Boundaries

To maintain solid relationship boundaries we need three skill sets, all of which have to be developed because no one is born with these skills. Unless we had the good fortune to have parents or mentors help us develop them when we were young, we must purposefully develop them as adults.

If we don't, they simply are not available to us to the degree they need to be for us to be as effective personally, professionally and in relationships as we could be. Personal and relationship boundaries are solid and healthy only to the degree that these skills are developed so it's important to have them.

The Three Skill Sets are:

1. **Assertiveness** – the ability to speak your truth, state your thoughts, feelings and position, and to disagree without intimidating or alienating others, and without allowing others to intimidate you. Assertiveness skills allow us to avoid being bullied or manipulated and to get what we want more consistently without imposing upon or taking advantage of others. If you need instruction in this area, a good place to begin is with the lessons on wikihow.com. Here's the link: http://www.wikihow.com/Be-Assertive-Without-Being-Arrogant.

2. **Persuasion** – a skill set based on effective communication and an understanding of motivation which allows you to positively influence others such that they are open to helping you achieve your goals. Effective persuasion leads people to *want* to help you. You can learn more about persuasion at wikihow.com. http://www.wikihow.com/Persuade-People

3. **Negotiation** – Negotiation is a skill set that is applied when persuasion fails to achieve the desired results. Negotiation is a means for getting what you want when people do *not* want to help you get it. Effective negotiation aims for win/win outcomes where each party gives up something they are willing to part with in order to gain something they want. Here's the wikihow.com link: http://www.wikihow.com/Negotiate

If you find it difficult to establish boundaries that prevent others from imposing upon you, or find that, in trying to get your needs met you upset or alienate others, you will greatly benefit from learning these three skill sets. If learning the basics online don't get you as far as you would like to go, consider getting a good coach. Be sure the one you choose is skilled in these three areas. You can find highly skilled coaches at www.quantumleapunuversity.org/search-coach.

All three skill sets are grounded in effective communication and are easier to develop for some people than for others because some people are naturally better communicators. Less than 12% of the population uses these skills effectively. Though they may look natural for the fortunate few who have mastered them, those people did *learn* them. We all have to since no one is born with them.

Take the time to create your boundaries and begin taking ownership of what's inside your circles. Until good, healthy personal boundaries are in place, the fifth factor, self-confidence, will not develop to healthy levels.

Remember: Building firm personal and relationship boundaries is not a one step process. As you continue to identify strengths you want to keep and limitations you want to eliminate, continue adding them to your charts.

If you find it difficult to establish boundaries that prevent others from imposing upon you or find that in trying to get your needs met, you upset or alienate others, you will greatly benefit from learning these three valuable skill sets. Begin with the journal prompts at www.quantumleapuniversity.org/journalprompts

If learning on your own doesn't get you as far as you would like to go, don't stay stuck. Do yourself a huge favor and invest in a good coach. Be sure the one you choose is skilled in these three areas and can get you where you want to go quickly. You can find exceptional coaches at Begin with the journal prompts at https://www.quantumleapuniversity.org/search-coach

We often hear phrases like "shoot for the moon" and "reach for the stars."

Do that...

But only after you are well-acquainted and deeply in love with the brilliant world you find inside yourself.

~Sherry Buffington~

CHAPTER SEVEN
Essential Number Five
Self-Confidence

Confidence is a stellar quality. Without it, we are hobbled no matter how much we know or how capable we could be if we had the courage to take action. Confidence gives us that courage. It's the "I can do it" quality that makes achieving the goals we set for ourselves possible. Wherever confidence exists—including *self*-confidence—three factors are always present: (1) knowledge, (2) experience and (3) positive feedback.

True confidence is not possible without all three factors. You can check the accuracy of this assertion by looking at any area of your life where you have confidence. In those areas, you will find *all three parts* of the confidence formula are present. You have sufficient knowledge. You have sufficient experience to validate the knowledge and know it can be depended upon, and the experience has made you proficient enough that you realize you are good at doing that particular thing, which is positive feedback. Where confidence is very high, you have likely also received positive feedback from others.

In areas where you *lack* confidence, you will always find that *one or more* of the three factors is *missing*. If you lack knowledge, you will also lack experience and positive feedback. We cannot gain experience without also gaining at least some degree of knowledge. We can gain knowledge without having any direct experience of it or without positive feedback to validate it, but it is then only knowledge and we have little confidence around it until it has been validated by experience and positive feedback.

Experience without knowledge can occur too, but we tend to gain knowledge along with experience and, until we do, confidence is low. Say, for example, that you decided to take up painting without taking lessons. In order to ever have any confidence as an artist, you would at least need to learn about the materials you will use. If you didn't you would experience a lot of failures and, if you didn't learn enough to succeed, you would eventually give up painting. Remember, we are motivated only by the need to move away from pain or toward pleasure.

Repeated failures are experienced as pain by the subconscious mind so you would eventually find painting undesirable.

Wherever you have considerable knowledge of something, but no confidence, you are either lacking sufficient experience to allow you to trust the knowledge, or you lack positive feedback, or both. You could study a sport like golf or tennis by reading books, watching movies, etc. for twenty years and know everything there is to know about it, for example, but until you actually *experienced* it and your experience yielded results good enough to convince you that you were capable of performing that activity well, there would be no confidence around performing that activity.

You might be very confident *talking* about it if you have experience discussing things and knew you were an able communicator, but despite all your confidence in discussing the activity, a request to actually *perform* it would strike terror in you because, in that arena, you would have no experience and no reason to believe you would get positive feedback from anyone.

Sometimes, people have sufficient knowledge and sufficient experience, but still don't get positive feedback. An example would be someone who has studied voice for years, has plenty of music knowledge, and has experience singing in private settings, but who has no natural talent for singing and cannot carry a tune. Even if such a person was deaf to her own poor performance, the negative feedback she would receive from others, verbally or non-verbally, would prevent confidence from developing fully.

Such an individual may charge forward declaring that they plan to become a rock star, and bravado may carry them forward for awhile. But bravado is not real. It cannot sustain an illusion for long, especially when the feedback is continually negative. In time the illusion must end. Those inclined to put on a show often blame others for their failures rather than admit that their false show of confidence *was* false and unsustainable.

Lack of internal positive feedback can prevent confidence from developing too. In this instance limiting beliefs prevent people who are actually proficient at a task from recognizing that fact. If you have ever tried to give a genuine compliment to someone who has low self-esteem, you know that insecure people don't accept compliments very well. Their false beliefs about their self (negative self-feedback) prevent them from seeing their truth.

When others compliment insecure people, the person being complimented either assumes the person giving the compliment is lying or is too blind to see the truth. Such individuals lack accurate knowledge about their self. They see themselves as lacking, and positive feedback from others is incongruent with their low self-image so they are unable to receive it.

The confidence formula is an invaluable tool for evaluating and correcting areas where you lack confidence. By referring to the formula, you can determine exactly what is lacking and what to focus on to get the desired result.

Confidence Formula

Knowledge
+
Experience
+
Positive Feedback
=
Confidence

When knowledge is the missing piece, usually the other two pieces are missing as well. Where you discover that knowledge is lacking, determine what you need to know and find a way to get that information. If you have plenty of knowledge in a particular area, but are still not confident, examine experience and feedback.

Salespeople are an interesting study in confidence. It is not uncommon for salespeople to have all kinds of knowledge around the products they sell and formal selling techniques, and still lack confidence. Sometimes the lack of confidence is a result of not having sufficient experience to qualify the knowledge they have gained. Sometimes confidence is lacking because the salesperson is receiving negative feedback from their manager or their prospects and don't have good personal boundaries to help them maintain a positive self-concept.

Sometimes they are comparing themselves to more effective salespeople and giving themselves negative feedback.

When people lack healthy personal boundaries, negative feedback from others generally increases self-doubt and fuels the negative feedback they give themselves.

Although being valued and accepted is a core need for all of us, the opinions of others have very little negative impact on us when we are sure of who we are and are not, where we stand, what we will and will not accept, and what we are capable of accomplishing.

Faith in what we are capable of accomplishing is the confidence piece, but we can't get there until we have the first four essential qualities developed, at least to some extent. To be sure of our capabilities and give ourselves honest positive feedback, we need to be *self-aware*, have a clear *sense of purpose* and *direction*, and *firm boundaries*. These provide the healthy sense of self upon which confidence is built.

Positive feedback, the third part of the confidence formula, can come from self or others. That which comes from self is most effective because it's self-sustaining. Without confidence, we accomplish very little and, without accomplishment, there can be no success.

Are you beginning to see how the first essential quality leads to the second; the second to the third; the third to the fourth, and so on?

To gain the many benefits you can get by moving through life confidently, confidence needs to be authentic and developed to a healthy level. You cannot fake confidence. Those who try are generally seen as arrogant rather than as confident.

When it is built on authentic self-awareness and healthy personal and relationship boundaries, and buoyed up by clarity around where you are headed in life, it is authentic and highly appealing, and it can get you very far in life.

Time to journal - www.quantumleapuniversity.org/journalprompts

CHAPTER EIGHT
Essential Number Six
Self-Esteem

Self-esteem is the quality that keeps us pushing past the challenges we face and moving steadily forward. It lets us know that we are worth whatever effort it takes to achieve our goals and realize our dreams.

Self-esteem is essential to success because, unless we believe we are worthy of the goals we set and the dreams we hold, we give up when things get tough. And whenever we are improving; gaining new skills or learning new, more successful strategies, we inevitably hit points on the learning curve where we face challenges.

All kinds of dreams fall by the wayside and many worthy goals are abandoned because low self-esteem has robbed the individual of the will to keep going. Self-esteem is absolutely essential for follow through. Without it we just buy the books, attend the seminars, join gyms, make New Year's resolutions, start the diets and fitness programs, and so on, but don't follow through to completion. Unless we believe we are *worth the effort,* we won't keep making the effort.

For self-esteem to develop, the first five essential qualities must be in place.

Five Steps to Self-esteem:
1. Before we believe we are worth the effort, we must love the self we know ourselves to be, and genuine self-love never grows around a false self. Self-esteem is a product of authenticity; of honoring ourselves and the attributes we were born with, and being tapped into our true passions (*Authentic Self-awareness*). Once we love who we are and what we are passionate about, we must align our goals with our true passion so we know where we are headed, and why (*Clear Purpose and Focus*).

2. Once we are clear on our passion, purpose and mission, and have a plan for traveling our own path successfully, we must believe that, if we follow our own authentic path, we will eventually realize our dream *(Open, Expectant, Positive Attitude and Beliefs)*.

3. As we step out onto our life path, we must be clear about who we are and what will keep us in integrity, and have the depth of awareness and strength of conviction to keep the agendas of others from pulling us off-course *(Solid, Healthy Boundaries)*.

4. Before we will seriously pursue our dream, we must believe we have the ability to overcome any challenges we encounter along the way *(Self-confidence)*.

5. We must believe we are worth whatever effort it takes to bring our dreams to fruition *(Self-esteem)*.

Let's use attempting to lose weight or get in shape as an example of failing because self-esteem is low. Self-esteem is not always the reason a diet fails, of course, but it is almost always what derails the effort. Generally, people go on a diet or begin an exercise routine because they want to look or feel better, but to succeed, a change in habits and routines must occur, and change brings up resistance in most people.

To get past the resistance requires effort and, just like climbing a progressively steeper slope, the farther we go into the endeavor, the greater our effort and determination must be to keep making progress, up to a certain point.

Once we have managed to get past the initial resistance, the new behaviors actually end up being much easier to sustain than the old, ineffective ones were. Before we can get to that place of ease however, we have to work through the resistance.

When we don't really believe we are worth the effort, there inevitably comes a point when the effort is greater than the value we place upon the outcome for ourselves and at that point, those without sufficient self-esteem give up.

Lack of self-esteem is generally the result of old childhood programs. Difficult circumstances or past failures can increase self-doubt, but its source can generally be traced back to the messages we bought into as children.

Efforts to gain self-esteem by changing external conditions almost never works. The beliefs we hold about ourselves have to change first. Willpower alone won't get the job done either, because willpower requires sticking to a new behavior and to do that, we have to believe we are worth the effort. If we don't have that belief by the time we reach our teens, developing it is a process that begins with a new view of who we are and what we are actually capable of, which is why the first five essential qualities must be developed first.

Failure to achieve most goals is not due to lack of capacity, but to lack of self-esteem. Everyone has the capacity to eat healthier foods and limit the intake of calories, and unless they are physically handicapped, everyone has the capacity to exercise. But physical capacity is not what decides how far we go in life and rarely is it our mental capacity. What decides our success is our emotional capacity.

Those who fail to do what they know they should, or who continue to do things they know they shouldn't, suffer from the most debilitating handicap on earth—and the most widespread. There is little to no sympathy for this great handicap either. In fact, most people don't even realize it exists because the people who suffer from it are often physically and mentally able. They are normally functioning people who appear to be perfectly capable of making and implementing good choices. Yet they consistently fail to do that.

The *effect* of this handicap is obvious, but the handicap itself is *invisible*, which is why people frequently fail to see or address it. And, because it is invisible, those who have it get lots of negative feedback from others and even from themselves. As a result, neither confidence nor self-esteem develops sufficiently.

This insidious, potential-destroying handicap is not a mental impairment, yet it affects mental activity in the form of beliefs and emotional blocks. It shuts people down, prevents them from doing the things they really would love to do, and keeps them doing things they would prefer to stop doing.

This handicap is thousands of times more prevalent than physical handicaps, yet it remains misunderstood and largely unseen. The most limiting handicap on earth is an emotional handicap.

Most often, the cause is childhood conditions that result in negative programming, but experiences later in life can be a cause too, especially when one or more of the essential qualities is undeveloped.

It is estimated that internal beliefs and limiting thoughts (all products of erroneous programming) make up 95% of what prevents people from achieving their goals. And the most common source of blocked potential is lack of self-awareness.

People who lack self-awareness also lack clarity, focus, purpose and a sense of direction. As a result, they keep heading down one wrong path after another, and keep getting unwanted results. People who lack self-awareness also lack personal and relationship boundaries so, in addition to not knowing where they need to be headed in life, they are being constantly thrown off-course by the imposed agendas of others, further ensuring that the results they get are not what they want.

Repeatedly getting unwanted results creates a negative feedback loop, which prevents self-confidence and self-esteem from developing—and the handicap grows larger.

This difficult cycle is hard to break without help. Almost no one succeeds at breaking it on their own and not just anyone can help. It has to be someone who understands the cycle and knows where to begin the healing process.

To keep going; to push past challenges and sustain the effort needed to reach the point where we are free to follow our own ideal path, we must *know* we are worth the effort, and those caught in the limitation trap don't know that.

Because clearing the old baggage is so crucial to unfettered progress, I spent years searching and researching ways to do that quickly, easily and permanently. I studied every quick response method I could find; Neuro-linguistic programming (NLP), the Silva Mind Method, Emotional Freedom Technique (EFT), and hypnotherapy to name a few. All have their benefits, but I found that all had limitations I wanted to eliminate. In some instances there were rituals, such as tapping, that turned some people off. The biggest problem though, was that the success rate for most of the methods was too low. I wanted something that worked as close to 100% of the time as possible so kept searching.

It was during my training in hypnotherapy that I discovered why most methods have limited success and I went to work to develop a method that would produce the kind of results I envisioned. The result is a method I call *Rapidly Accelerated Mind Patterning* (RAMP). I chose that name because deeply ingrained patterns are the source of most difficult-to-change mental and emotional blocks, and the ones most other methods don't affect. Most of the other modalities are effective at reducing stress and eliminating some habits, but ingrained patterns which develop around long-repeated habits, are harder to alter or eliminate than habits and require a different approach. You can learn more about RAMP at www.banishblocks.com

Why Patterns Form

To increase effectiveness and conserve energy, the mind automates repeated thoughts and actions by forming habits. Once a habit is formed, no conscious thought is required to repeat the action. This not only speeds up response time, it also conserves energy since conscious thought increases brain activity which burns more energy.

Habits that are repeated over time form well established synaptic pathways which form patterns that are laid down like a blueprint which the mind follows consistently. The ingrained patterns all have a perceived purpose and are impossible to change at a conscious level. Even typical therapy doesn't affect established patterns when the source cause is not consciously accessible, as is often the case. And even when the source cause is known, changing established patterns can take years with traditional methods. It isn't uncommon for people who seek help to report that they have been in therapy for years, sometimes ten or more, and the limiting patterns are still there.

Time is far too precious to allow years to pass without real progress, but to make progress, the old patterns that keep us stuck have to be altered or eliminated. Many people are able to alter old patterns by beginning with self-awareness and progressively developing each of the seven essential qualities.

Start at the beginning and go as far as you can on your own. You may be surprised at how quickly you progress. If you are steadily moving toward your goals and dreams, just keep going. But, if you get stuck and are not progressing, don't spend years trying to get past a block.

Be willing to invest in a method that will help you get unstuck and moving forward again.

If self-administered methods, such as EFT work for you, use those. If you aren't familiar with EFT, you can find lots of instructions on the internet.

If, after doing all you can on your own, you are still stuck, consider investing in a RAMP session. The RAMP method eliminates blocks and gets the desired result more than 97% of the time in as little as an hour. And once a change is made, the feelings and behaviors associated with the old pattern immediately disappear and are replaced with new beneficial behaviors which are effortless to sustain. Learn more about the RAMP method at www.banishblocks.com or, if you want to schedule a session with a Quantum Leap Coach, go to www.quantumleapuniversity.org/search-coach and select a RAMP coach.

Time to journal - www.quantumleapuniversity.org/journalprompts

According to the laws of physics,
The bumblebee shouldn't fly.
Perhaps it's nature's way of saying
You can do anything if you try.

~Sherry Buffington~

CHAPTER NINE
Essential Number Seven
Effective Self-Management

Self-management is characterized by the ability to cope with stressors effectively, have the discipline to defer gratification in order to do the right thing and stay focused on the long term effect, and to act responsibly and courageously so what we do from moment to moment will have a positive impact now and into the future. It is through effective self-management that we are able to express our finest talents and our particular kind of genius, and though it never develops to highly effective levels until the other six qualities are in place, once they are in place, it tends to develop naturally and with relative ease.

Greatness is never achieved by irresponsible, undisciplined people who lack the courage of their convictions, which is why self-management is essential to lasting success. Until we are able to manage our behaviors and the emotions that drive them effectively, we either wander through life like rudderless ships, blown about by the winds of circumstance, or we are in a constant battle trying to hold our ground. In either case, we are ineffective at directing our lives purposefully and generally end up anywhere but where we want to be.

There are emotionally immature people who, on the surface, appear to be successful, but if you look closer, you'll find that they either gained their position on the coat tail of someone else (usually wealthy parents or a wealthy spouse) or are leading train-wreck lives behind the scenes. I have never known a truly successful person who just fell into the perfect circumstance. Even if someone did happen to luck into success, the likelihood of sustaining it without effective self-management is pretty slim. Mismanaged lives generally lead to ever increasing misery, not to increasing success.

Effective self-management is *in part* what author Daniel Goleman called *Emotional Intelligence* or EQ. Much research has been done around this important factor and the research consistently validates the many benefits that can be derived from emotional intelligence.

Some studies suggest that EQ is the number one factor for achieving success personally, professionally and in relationships. As a result, many people try to begin here, and they generally fail because EQ is not the whole package.

There is no question that emotional intelligence is vitally important. In fact, it's essential to lasting success. But it's one of seven essential qualities, not a stand-alone end all. Trying to develop EQ without first developing the other factors is an exercise in frustration and futility as many organizations have discovered to their dismay when they have tried to solve personnel problems purely from an EQ perspective.

The EQ Model has Four Main Constructs:

1. **Self-awareness** – this is generally applied to self-awareness as it affects *emotional* responses, which is only part of the picture, but here it is again as the number one factor. Self-awareness as it is applied to EQ is the ability to comprehend and accurately assess one's own emotions and to recognize their impact on others. It also refers to the ability to use intuition or "gut feelings" to guide decisions.

2. **Self-management** – this refers to the ability to control one's own emotions and impulses, and to adapt effectively to changing circumstances.

3. **Social awareness** – this is the ability to sense, understand, and properly react to other people's emotions, to comprehend the structure and purpose of social networks, and to function effectively within them.

Relationship management – this refers to the ability to inspire, influence and develop others, and effectively manage conflict.

Each construct in Goleman's model includes a set of emotional competencies which Goleman correctly asserts are *learned* capabilities, not innate talents. Emotional intelligence skills are indeed learned, but only people who have already developed the other essential qualities develop them to highly effective levels.

Few people develop the qualities necessary for effective self-management as children. The few who develop them generally do so as adults, and most are in their thirties before they begin.

Unfortunately, most people never develop them to highly effective levels. Even top officials running companies and politicians running countries often lack emotional intelligence. This fact is woefully obvious to anyone who watches the proceedings of the U.S. senators and congressmen.

One reason so few have developed emotional intelligence and so many find developing it difficult is because effective self-management cannot be developed independent of the other essential qualities because they are the framework upon which self-management rests and through which it develops.

Organizations spend millions of dollars on EQ training each year with little effect. Studies show that the range of improvement is between 11% and 24%. The reason the results aren't better is because the majority of the people who go through EQ training don't have the other essential qualities developed. It's a cart before the horse effect. The average of the 11-24% range is 16.5%, which means that, on average, EQ does not improve significantly in 83.5% of trainees. Remember the research I mentioned in chapter 3 which suggests that 84% of the U.S. population don't know themselves well enough to report accurately on a personality assessment? There is a very close correlation between the two percentages that speaks volumes and points to the extreme importance of developing self-awareness and the other essential qualities.

If you have ever tried to will yourself to be more patient with people who rub you the wrong way, you know how difficult it is to change an emotional response without changing your perception of yourself or the other person. That is essentially how futile it is to try to develop emotional intelligence without first developing the foundation for it.

Advice on developing emotional intelligence is primarily around managing emotions, which you will definitely want to do, even before you have the other essentials in place, though you'll find you progress a lot faster and easier once they are.

To Develop Effective Self-Management:

1. **Notice your emotional reactions** to events throughout the day. Take time to acknowledge how you feel about your experiences. If you ignore your feelings, you will miss important information that has a direct effect on your mindset and the way you behave. Connecting your feelings to experiences will raise your awareness and improve your EQ. Make a habit of tapping into your emotions at certain times every day until you become accustomed to noticing them. Try asking yourself, "what put me there?"

2. **Notice how your body responds** to different emotions. Every emotion creates a physical manifestation which acts as an early warning system when you are paying attention. Once you recognize your physiological response to an emotion, you can use that response to get negative emotions in check before they spiral out of control. Especially notice how your body responds to fear, anger, frustration, anxiety, depression, sadness and stress. Managing these early will give you many advantages. For example, fear might show up as a knot in your stomach, or tightness in your chest, or sweaty palms, or quick, shallow breathing. Sadness often shows up as a feeling of heaviness where happiness is generally described as a feeling of lightness. As you attend to your body's responses, you'll discover that it responds to particular emotions in the same way every time. This is that perfect inner-compass working to help you stay on track. Pay attention to it.

3. **Observe how you tend to act** in response to your emotions. The better you understand how your emotions affect your behavioral impulses, the more control you will have over your responses. For example, maybe you raise your voice when you are angry or clam up when you feel uncertain. When you're feeling overwhelmed, you might sigh a lot or start multi-tasking to the point of losing focus. Knowing your typical response gives you the opportunity to anticipate it and choose a better one.

4. **Allow and learn from your emotions** rather than judging them. All emotions have a purpose. Every one of them provides valuable feedback, including the negative ones. If you allow some feelings and suppress others, you will limit your ability to live fully and you will miss important feedback. Effective self-management isn't about suppressing or disallowing negative emotions, it's about

managing them. The emotion is never the problem. It's what we do with it. For example, you can feel anger and start yelling at people, or you can feel it and recognize that it's there because you feel passionate about something. With that recognition, you then have the opportunity to explore the passion and use it to your advantage.

5. **Practice choosing your responses.** Rather than trying to control your emotions, (which is a losing proposition) work on controlling your responses. Choose an emotion that you don't generally manage very well and decide how you are going to behave next time it comes up. Once you have mastered the big one, mastering all the others will be easy.

6. **Use the 90 Second Rule.** The 90 Second Rule was introduced by Dr. Jill Bolte Taylor, a brain scientist at Harvard Medical School. She found that emotions create loops in the amygdala circuitry of the brain which keeps cycling as long as we hold onto the emotion, and that with each loop the brain speeds the process exponentially so that by the fifth repetition, the loop is traveling 16 times faster than in the first loop. The effect is that the energy of the emotion we are holding onto gets bigger and more powerful, and soon we are out of control of it.

Dr. Taylor also found that when a person has an emotional reaction to something in their environment, there's a 90 second chemical process that happens in the body and which carries the emotion and creates a physiological response. After the chemical process dissipates, which it always does within 90 seconds, the automatic response is over and any remaining emotional response is just the person choosing to stay in that emotional loop.

If the individual holds onto the emotion beyond the 90 seconds, the emotional loop starts cycling faster and faster, intensifying the emotion with each cycle. At that point, the amygdala hijacks your brain and you are out of control.

To apply the 90 Second Rule, notice your physiological response, take a few deep breaths (deep breathing delivers oxygen to the brain and calms the body), and acknowledge the emotion.

For example, you might say, "I am feeling anxious" or "I am starting to get angry." Labeling feelings engages the prefrontal cortex which acts as a suppressant to the amygdala and weakens the response.

Then purposefully reframe your assessment of the situation seeking a more positive frame of reference. This helps you let go of the feeling so that you are not feeding the amygdala after the 90 seconds have passed. This method works miracles for managing emotions.

7. **Practice empathy, understanding and emotional honesty.** Notice how others are feeling and let people know how you are feeling being sure to be tactful and considerate as you do. Being open and honest builds trust and lets you come across as more genuine and approachable. Pay attention to the effect you have on others as well as the effect they have on you.

8. **Realize there is always room for improvement.** Consider patterns you might need to change. Emotional patterns create relationship dynamics. To improve a relationship, change any negative patterns you bring into it. Since we all have blind spots, ask people you trust to give you honest feedback on your emotional responses and patterns.

Effective self-management isn't as hard as most people make it seem. In fact, once you are on your ideal path, with a clear vision of where you are headed; once you expect good things to happen, have good, solid personal and relationship boundaries so others can't pull you off your path; and once you are confident and know you are worthy of the best life has to offer, effective-self management is as easy as deciding to be your best and share your best qualities with others.

Time to journal - www.quantumleapuniversity.org/journalprompts

CHAPTER TEN
Creating Your Path to Success

Once you know what energizes and motivates you, start adding details to the basic plan you laid out as you worked through the second essential, clear purpose and focus. This brings your own personal brand of success into better focus and gives you a target at which to aim.

It might be tempting to try to by-pass the planning step because laying out a plan takes time and can feel like a barrier to progress. Don't fall into that trap. Your plan acts as a road map and, although creating it takes time, having it will help you stay on track and will greatly increase your progress. Not having a plan to follow almost always results in delays, *not* in greater progress.

You only need the first three essential qualities in place before you lay out your plan. You can develop the others as you move forward. You'll need to get your boundaries in place as soon as possible so others don't push their agendas off on you and hinder your progress, but you don't need to wait until all seven essential qualities are developed before you get started. Start where you are, do what you can, use what you have and enjoy the journey. Just don't make the mistake of expecting to gain and maintain success without having the seven essential qualities in place.

If leaping into action unprepared or just gathering information were enough, we could all read a few good books, jump into the arena, and become everything we ever wanted to be. But, as you know, it doesn't work that way. Do the *internal* work so you are well prepared to succeed.

The Final Factors

Besides the seven essentials, there are four other factors that will greatly impact your outcomes and affect your ability to gain and maintain lasting success. The first one typically develops along with the seven essentials. That isn't necessarily true for the other three.

These are not presented as essentials for success because there are people who achieve success in some areas of life without them. When the first of the four factors, money mindset, is not present, success is usually gained in areas other than money. When the other three are missing, success is generally strictly financial, and often doesn't last.

Though success on some levels is possible without having these qualities in place, I don't know of a single person that is truly successful overall (financially, in relationships, in maintaining health, and in personal satisfaction and happiness) without these factors, however. For complete and *lasting* success, these must be developed as well.

The Additional Qualities are:
- Money Mindset
- Values
- Principles
- Ethics

Money Mindset

One of the biggest blocks for most people is around money. Approximately 97% of the population has unproductive beliefs about money so the likelihood that you do is immense. Even the few who have managed to eliminate the negative messages and replace them with wealth-producing ones are regularly exposed to a lot of negative messages from others, which can have an adverse effect. So being fully conscious of your money messages and keeping them tuned toward wealth is vital. To help you uncover any unproductive beliefs you might have, complete the following two exercises.

What does money mean to you?

Money is our primary medium of exchange and, as such, it has many meanings. The meanings we attach to money directly affect the relationship we have with it and dictate how we feel about it. By understanding what money means to you, you will be in a better position to speed your progress.

Money Exercise 1

From the list below, choose what you believe to be the five most important applications for money, ranking them from 1 to 5 with *1 being most important* and *5 being least important.*

___1. Comfort – A means for avoiding pain; a life of ease

___2. Freedom – Greater variety; a means for increasing choices

___3. Survival – Food, clothing, shelter

___4. Security – Adequate funds to feel safe and avoid worry

___5. Stability – Greater predictability over time; constancy

___6. Significance – A way to gain importance or accomplish something grand

___7. Pleasure – A ticket to fun, travel, hobbies, play

___8. Power – A means for gaining control; a way to win, to keep score

___9. Prestige – Influence; respect; a visible measure of success

___10. Love – A way to take care of others, to do good

___11. Self-Growth – A means to improve and expand potential

___12. Worthiness – An affirmation of worth and value

___13. Independence – To be financially self-sufficient

___14. Compensation - Payment for time and effort

___15. Unimportant – Money does not matter

Money Exercise 2

Below is a list of 40 common messages around money. Rate yourself on a scale from 0 – 5 on each of the following statements, with *0 being totally disagree* and *5 being totally agree.*

___ 1. Money is the root of all evil.

___ 2. Most rich people are not happy or content.

___ 3. Most rich people probably got their money by being ruthless.

___ 4. Having a lot of money might make me less spiritual.

___ 5. Getting rich takes a lot of hard work.

___ 6. Having a lot of money is a big responsibility.

___ 7. I don't have what it takes to get really rich.

___ 8. Realistically, I will probably never be rich.

___ 9. Getting rich requires luck; being in the right place at the right time.

___ 10. Big money does not come to ordinary people like me.

___ 11. Striving for wealth won't allow much time for anything else in life.

___ 12. To be rich, you have to take advantage of people.

___ 13. If I get rich, everyone will want something from me.

___ 14. If I get rich there are people in my life who won't like it.

___ 15. If I have a lot of money, it means someone else has less.

___ 16. People who amass more money than they need are greedy.

___ 17. Money intimidates me. I'm not very good at financial stuff.

___ 18. If I get a lot of money, I might lose it and be disappointed in myself.

___ 19. If I really try to gain wealth and don't succeed, I'll feel like a failure.

___ 20. I have the potential for wealth; all I need is a break.

___ 21. This just isn't the right time for me to start "going for it, financially."

___ 22. I don't really want to be rich.

___ 23. Money isn't really that important.

___ 24. You can't pursue wealth and personal fulfillment at the same time.

___ 25. Money can cause a lot of problems.

___ 26. It's presumptuous to think I can earn more than my parents did.

___ 27. I would dishonor my parents if I tried to be wealthier than them.

___ 28. People never get rich doing only what they love.

___ 29. It takes money to make money.

___ 30. People don't need more money than it takes to live comfortably.

___ 31. Striving for big money can cause stress and health problems.

___ 32. It's difficult to get rich these days.

___ 33. Most of the good opportunities are gone.

___ 34. Given my past, it would be difficult for me to get rich.

___ 35. I'm not smart, intelligent or educated enough to get rich.

___ 36. I'm too young to get rich, people won't take me seriously.

___ 37. I'm too old to get rich. I don't have the time and energy.

___ 38. You have to sell to be rich and I don't like selling or promoting.

___ 39. Financial security comes from having a good job and a steady paycheck.

___ 40. I don't have time to manage money.

Examine Strong Responses

Go back through the statements and notice the ones with a ranking of 5 or zero. Both scores indicate a strong emotional response. Realize that *nothing gets your attention unless it impacts your subconscious mind* in some way. Whether you strongly agree or strongly disagree with a statement, it impacts you in some way. You can gain insights into your beliefs whether a statement feels like a truth or something you strongly reject. In the case of a statement you reject, look for beliefs you hold that cause you to reject the statement. Usually these are beneficial beliefs which can be used to negate some of the negative ones.

You may want to go through each of the statements you have checked with a friend, mentor or coach to discover your overall money pattern. Awareness is the first step to changing concepts and, changing concepts often changes behaviors.

If, after working through the money messages and discovering your patterns, you are unable to eliminate a belief or pattern, get help. A trained coach can help you eliminate money blocks, reframe beliefs and rewrite messages that are keeping you stuck below your potential.

Values

Values are broad-based beliefs in which we are deeply invested. The level of importance we place on family over work, or work over family, for example, is based on the values we hold. How honest we are, and under which circumstances, the principles we adhere to and what we consider ethical and unethical are also based in values.

Values, principles and ethics inform our choices, determine our direction in life and strongly influence the nature of our goals and dreams. To demonstrate how values, principles and ethics influence our choices and behaviors, I will use an example everyone is familiar with—human life.

Those who don't value human life, have no problem killing people. Those who highly value it, would never dream of killing anyone under any circumstance. The way each person approaches the subject of human life and what they do with it is based on *values*.

Principles

Principles differ from values in that they define the rules or codes of conduct by which we remain true to the values we hold. For example, honor can exist among thieves whose principles dictate that they not steal from their family or friends. In this case, only strangers are at risk. Where principles don't exclude family and friends, everyone is at risk.

Ethics

Ethics deal with morality and what we consider good or bad and right or wrong to do. Ethics drive *opinions*, but not actions. Actions are driven by *values* due to the emotional attachment to the belief.

Going back to those who value life, let's see how the three factors unfold. We will start with three people who highly value life, each with different principles in relation to that value. The principle or rule for the first person is that no one should ever kill anyone under any circumstance. The rule for the second person is that good people should never be killed, but bad people deserve to die. The rule for the third person is that life includes more than just physical existence and extends to individual rights and opinions.

Based on these rules, the first person would not kill anyone even if they believed not doing so would result in their own death or the death of a loved one. Many such people won't even kill a bug.

The second person would have no problem killing someone they perceived as bad or evil, but would never kill someone they believed was good and virtuous. The Kansas man that killed a doctor who ran an abortion clinic had this rule. In his mind, the doctor was killing innocent babies (good people) and was therefore a bad person that deserved to die. The belief that the doctor was doing something wrong and was bad for what he was doing was an ethically based (moral) opinion. The strong value around life for the good and innocent is what drove the behavior.

The third person would be more likely to take a "live and let live" approach. This person would never do anything as radical as killing an abortion doctor even if he disagreed with the practice. This person's beliefs allow for the doctor's right to have a different opinion or take a different action.

Ethics accurately reflect principles (or codes of conduct) and principles accurately reflect values, though this is not always apparent.

For example, religious leaders that don't practice what they preach espouse principles they don't personally adhere to. Whether they are sexually abusing congregation members, having illicit affairs, stealing from the coffers, or doing anything else which is contrary to what they preach, we can know that they don't really *value* what they preach.

What they value is *self-satisfaction*. Their public image is just a persona. It is *not* who they really are. The public ethics they preach are just part of the job. They preach what they believe people want to hear and what will keep their church populated, but their private values and principles are what determine their ethics and drive their behind the scenes behaviors.

When the value is self-satisfaction, the principles that define their code of conduct are essentially "if it feels good, do it." Their ethic says they can practice self-satisfaction and do what feels good as long as the action remains private and hidden from scrutiny, and does not result in lack of self-satisfaction (which exposure would do). It's a "what others don't know won't hurt them (or me)" philosophy. Even the act of becoming a preacher feeds the value of self-satisfaction for such people in that this job allows those so inclined to be revered as the voice of God.

People are always true to their real values no matter what they espouse, and because this is so, you can learn a lot about people by looking beyond what they say and noticing what they do. By noticing *actions* rather than words, you can also determine how well (or poorly) the seven essential qualities are developed in anyone, including yourself.

Our consistent behaviors determine our outcomes, and how well we have developed the seven essentials determines what we will consistently do.

Throughout this book I have stressed the importance of developing the essentials in the order in which they have been presented. I have pointed out that the very first essential, the foundation upon which all the others rest, is authentic self-awareness and expression.

Shakespeare wrote *"This above all: to thine own self be true, and it must follow, as the night the day, thou canst not then be false to any man."* I have found this to be true time and time again. It is not possible to hide behind a façade and still be authentic. To be authentic, you have to be *real* and the way you live your life and express yourself must accurately reflect the real you.

Those who fail to honor their own authentic self also fail to honor others and that house of cards is bound to come tumbling down eventually no matter how powerful an individual is or how much money they have amassed. History is full of stories of people with power, position and money who ultimately failed – Napoleon, Hitler, Bernie Madoff (the ponzi scheme thief), Kenneth Lay and Jeffrey Skilling (who rose to the top of the Enron Corporation and made a fortune duping other people before their scheme fell apart) are just a few.

All of these people had strong egos, but not a strong sense of their authentic self and certainly not good ethics. They had the often touted can-do attitude and appeared to strongly believe in themselves, though this was a façade. They developed certain leadership traits (though not to healthy levels), they had personal boundaries that prevented others from infringing upon them (never mind that they infringed upon others), and they had plenty of confidence in their ability to pull off something grand. But they lacked much more than they possessed.

They lacked authenticity and real self-esteem, though they covered that fact with bravado. Clearly they believed they were worth the effort needed to amass money and success, and apparently they had no problem looking in the mirror each day and being okay with what they saw. They thought they had clarity around what they wanted to accomplish, but failed to look beyond personal desires to see the long-term effect. And since effective self-management includes acting responsibly and with consideration, crooks and tyrants definitely lack that.

People such as these prove that monetary success is possible without upright values, principles or ethics. But winning the power game or the money game and losing self-respect, self-esteem, and the respect and esteem of others, is a hollow victory.

Values, principles and ethics are to overall abundance and success what nutrition is to the human body. The body can sustain itself for a very long time without good nutrition, but eventually the body begins to break down, falls ill and dies. The same holds true for what appears to be worldly success. The facade can be sustained for quite some time before things begin to fall apart. But you can be sure that where values, principles and ethics are lacking, what you see on the outside is a fragile illusion. On the inside things are slowly (or perhaps rapidly) falling apart and, in time, are bound to fall apart.

Core Values Exercise:

To help you identify your core values, I have provided a rather substantial list for you to explore. There are a total of 120 values listed. I listed that many so you can uncover important *themes*. Themes drive our decisions and when you understand what yours are you can purposefully align your goals with them and enjoy faster progress and greater satisfaction.

As you work through this exercise, you will discover that the values you check have commonalities, and those commonalities fit within one to three major categories or themes. You can learn a great deal about yourself, your choices and the best direction for you to take going forward by understanding the themes that define your beliefs.

STEP ONE – Choose Your Values

Scan through the list of values and check the *twenty* that are most important to you. You might want to use a pencil so you can alter your selections or pare them down to twenty if too many have high appeal. It helps to read through the list first so you know what's there. Values are all positive so you may find a lot of them appealing. Be selective. Out of 120 options, you only want to end up with twenty.

1. ____ Abundance/Wealth
2. ____ Acceptance/Appreciation
3. ____ Accomplishment/Achievement/Drive
4. ____ Accuracy/Precision
5. ____ Action/Results/Challenge
6. ____ Adaptability/Flexibility
7. ____ Adventure/Exploration/Discovery
8. ____ Affection/Kindness/Approachability
9. ____ Affluence/Position
10. ____ Altruism/Generosity/Selflessness
11. ____ Acknowledgment
12. ____ Assertiveness/Assurance
13. ____ Attractiveness/Beauty
14. ____ Balance
15. ____ Being the Best/Excellence
16. ____ Belonging/ Camaraderie/Friendship
17. ____ Boldness/Confidence/Bravery

18. ____ Candor/Frankness/ Straight Talk
19. ____ Capability/Effectiveness
20. ____ Carefulness/Certainty
21. ____ Celebrity/Fame
22. ____ Charisma/Charm
23. ____ Chastity/Purity
24. ____ Cheerfulness
25. ____ Clarity/Vision
26. ____ Closeness/Caring/Devotion
27. ____ Comfort
28. ____ Commitment
29. ____ Companionship/Connection
30. ____ Compassion/Empathy
31. ____ Compliance/Obedience/ Humility
32. ____ Consistency/Continuity
33. ____ Contentment/Satisfaction
34. ____ Contribution
35. ____ Control (of outcomes)
36. ____ Correctness
37. ____ Courage/Daring/Heroism
38. ____ Courtesy/Thoughtfulness
39. ____ Creativity
40. ____ Credibility
41. ____ Dependability/Timeliness
42. ____ Devoutness/Spirituality
43. ____ Dignity

44. ____ Discipline/Responsibility
45. ____ Discretion/Discernment
46. ____ Dominance/Control (of others)
47. ____ Duty
48. ____ Education/Knowledge/Learning
49. ____ Efficiency/Expertise/Mastery
50. ____ Enjoyment/Fun/Excitement
51. ____ Entertainment/Leisure/Amusement
52. ____ Fairness/Cooperation
53. ____ Faithfulness/Fidelity
54. ____ Family
55. ____ Financial Independence/Wealth
56. ____ Fitness/Health/Longevity
57. ____ Focus/Direction/Independence
58. ____ Freedom/Liberty
59. ____ Friendliness/Helpfulness
60. ____ Frugality/Thriftiness/Economy
61. ____ Gratitude/Thankfulness
62. ____ Growth/Personal Development
63. ____ Harmony/Peacefulness
64. ____ Holiness/Righteousness/Reverence
65. ____ Honesty/Truth/Sincerity
66. ____ Hygiene/Cleanliness
67. ____ Ingenuity/Inventiveness
68. ____ Insightfulness/Imagination
69. ____ Integrity

70. ____ Intelligence/Brilliance
71. ____ Intuitiveness/Inspiration
72. ____ Justice
73. ____ Leadership
74. ____ Logic
75. ____ Love/Intimacy
76. ____ Loyalty/Honor
77. ____ Making a Difference/Significance
78. ____ Mastery/Precision
79. ____ Maturity
80. ____ Modesty
81. ____ Money/Wealth/Prosperity
82. ____ Open-mindedness
83. ____ Optimism
84. ____ Order/Organization/Neatness
85. ____ Originality/Uniqueness
86. ____ Persuasiveness/Power
87. ____ Poise/Polish/Refinement
88. ____ Popularity
89. ____ Practicality/Pragmatism/Prudence
90. ____ Preparedness
91. ____ Privacy
92. ____ Professionalism
93. ____ Reliability
94. ____ Resourcefulness
95. ____ Recognition/Respect

96. _____ Security
97. _____ Self-control
98. _____ Self-reliance
99. _____ Sensuality/Sexuality
100. _____ Service
101. _____ Sharing
102. _____ Significance
103. _____ Simplicity
104. _____ Solitude/Tranquility
105. _____ Spirituality
106. _____ Spontaneity
107. _____ Stability
108. _____ Strength
109. _____ Structure
110. _____ Success/Winning
111. _____ Sympathy/Support
112. _____ Teamwork/Synergy
113. _____ Thoroughness
114. _____ Thoughtfulness
115. _____ Tidiness/Cleanliness
116. _____ Trust/Trustworthiness
117. _____ Usefulness/Utility
118. _____ Variety/Flexibility
119. _____ Vigor/Vitality/Health/Youthfulness
120. _____ Wisdom

STEP TWO – Discover Your Themes

Now go back through the values you selected and combine similar words into themes by looking for commonalities. Record the overall themes below. If, for example, you selected "making a difference; importance", "service", "altruism; generosity" and "sympathy; support", those words would combine into a theme of "Selfless Service." If you selected "leadership", "making a difference in the world", "significance" "persuasiveness; and "power," even though both sets contain "Making a difference in the world" your theme around how you would do that is quite different. Here the theme implies the importance of being a leader.

Themes

1. _____
2. _____
3. _____

STEP THREE – Rank the Themes

If you have more than one theme, rank them according to their importance to you. Then choose the most important one. If you could only live within one theme, which would it be?

Primary Theme: _____

STEP FOUR – Determine Your Core Values

From the values that make up your themes, choose the three that are *most important* to you. You can select values from each of the themes to arrive at the three most important.

There might be two values in one theme and one in another. Or they may all be in the same theme. The more core values a theme contains, the more significant that theme is to your sense of well being. Prioritize your top three values and list them in order of priority. The value in doing this is that you can use your most important core values to guide your decisions as you build your ideal life.

Core Values

1. _____

2. _____

3. _____

STEP FIVE – Rules, Codes of Conduct and Morality

After you have narrowed your choices down to the three core values, try to discover the principles (rules and codes of conduct) and ethics (moral aspects) contained in them.

Once you have completed this exercise, check to see if the *beliefs* you hold and which sustain your core values, principles or ethics, conflict with your idea of success.

If you find a belief that isn't serving you well, you can always change it, but to change beliefs at the values level you must address the *emotional connection* to it and then reframe your broad based view or assumption in order to change the *emotion*. Beliefs can also be changed at the *principles* level by rewriting the rules.

If you decide to change a belief at the principles level, be sure the new rules do not conflict with the emotional aspect of the belief. If it conflicts, the change will not occur or if change occurs, it will not last.

Let's use the value of respect from others as an example to demonstrate changing a value by changing the *emotion* attached to it. People who have weak personal boundaries are often offended by others and feel disrespected. They respond to the feeling of being disrespected by feeling hurt and withdrawing or by getting angry and lashing out. Neither response is beneficial for building healthy relationships.

To change the reaction, the *belief* must change. The *value* (wanting respect from others) does not change, but the belief can. Personal boundaries help a lot here. They create a layer of insulation which leads to greater self-esteem and the belief that you are *worthy* of being respected.

From a place of worthiness you are more likely to respond to someone who acts disrespectfully with the assumption that the person is having a bad day or doesn't have very good interpersonal skills. Their disrespect is then about *them*, not about you, and you are better able to deal with it appropriately.

Again, using respect as an example, let's see how a belief can be changed by changing the *rules* around that value. People, who get easily upset when others disrespect them, typically have more than just weak personal boundaries. They also have rules of conduct that say people *should* respect one another. Or, as least they have a rule that says people should respect *them*, whether or not the respect is earned.

By creating a new rule which states that people should only respect one another when respect has been *earned*, disrespect then gets a different response. Instead of being automatically mad when someone acts disrespectful, we now look at *ourselves* to see whether we have earned that person's respect. If we discover we have not earned respect, and also have a rule that says we should learn from our mistakes, we would then use the opportunity to correct our behaviors. If we determine we earned respect, but didn't get it, the rule we apply to that scenario would determine our response.

STEP SIX – Apply Rules and Beliefs

Examine the rules, codes of conduct and beliefs around each of your Core Values.

If you discover rules or beliefs that are preventing you from being as effective as you want to be, REWRITE them. You will be amazed at how quickly your actions and outcomes change when the rules you live by change.

VALUE #1 _____

Rules for this value

Codes of conduct for this value (how you and others should behave):

Beliefs around this value:

VALUE #2 _____

Rules for this value:

Codes of conduct for this value (how you and others should behave):

Beliefs around this value:

VALUE #3 _____

Rules for this value:

Codes of conduct for this value (how you and others should behave):

Beliefs around this value:

CHAPTER ELEVEN
Wrapping It All Up

Every truly successful person I have ever met has all seven of the essential qualities in place, and every unsuccessful person has one or more of them missing or undeveloped—sometimes most or all of them.

Nothing you can invest in will bring you greater rewards or a greater return on your investment than developing the seven essential qualities and shoring them up with a healthy money mindset and good values, principles and ethics.

We have covered how each of the qualities builds on the others as we progressed through them. To see how they work together to build a solid foundation upon which to create lasting success, let's do a quick review.

Essential Step One: Authentic Self-awareness and Expression

Find your true self and learn to express it authentically. Once you do, your passion and your ideal path will become apparent and you will have constancy (your own True North) that nothing in the outside world can take away from you. In an ever changing, fast-paced world, having an unchanging sense of self is one of the greatest treasures you could possibly have. With a solid sense of self, no matter what life throws at you, you can always find your way back home. You will find your true passion at the core of your authentic self too, and passion is the source of the much touted success attribute of persistence.

From your authentic self comes the external success drivers of constancy, passion, persistence, and motivation.

Essential Step Two: Clear Purpose and Focus

Once you have that unchangeable personal core and the passion that flows from it, decide how you will build your future around them so you are moving steadily toward goals that bring the things most important to you into fruition. When you are clear about what gives your life purpose and meaning, staying true to your purpose will help you make decisions that lead you ever closer to a successful, fulfilled life.

From clear purpose and focus come the external success drivers of direction, determination, good decision-making, structure, planning, goal setting, and vision.

Begin Where You Are

Your authentic path is the only one you can count on for lasting success. Start constructing it now. You may not have all the details yet, but describing your ideal life in writing and in as much detail as you can will guide your decisions and help you stay on course as you develop the other success qualities. You can add details as you go along.

Eventually, the picture you create needs to be so complete and so clear in your mind that you are able to experience the life you want in *as much detail* as the life you are currently living. Also (and this is very important) the life you are moving toward needs to have a *greater emotional component* than the life you now have. It needs to feel so real that you are able to take complete *ownership* of it.

The reason this is so vitally important is because the subconscious mind attends to whatever has the most clarity and emotional energy around it. So if you have more clarity and energy attached to your current circumstances than you do to your ideal, your subconscious mind will work 24/7 to maintain your current circumstances.

The reason you need to take ownership of your ideal life as soon as you have defined it, is because the subconscious mind lives in the here and now. It doesn't concern itself with the future. So, as long as you keep the realization of your goals and dreams in the future, your subconscious mind will not act upon them. Though you are setting completion dates in the future, you need to *own the outcome now*.

Not taking ownership of outcomes in the here and now is the primary reason goals are not achieved. Crisis workers who defer action and then are able to get so much done in a pinch, can do that because they have taken ownership of the crisis which signals the subconscious mind to leap into action. Imagine what you could get done if your powerful subconscious mind was working for you right from the start. That's what happens when you take ownership of an outcome.

Once your ideal life is clear and present in your mind, decide what steps you need to take and in which order. Be sure the steps are doable. If you make your goal steps too grand and fail to achieve them, your subconscious mind will associate goal setting with failure, and will avoid it. If the goal steps are small and doable, and regularly result in success, your subconscious mind will associate goal setting with success and you will find setting and achieving goals easier and a lot more fun. Once goal setting is associated with success, you can set larger goals and move forward faster. It's important to have goal achievement connected to success so be sure your early goals are very doable.

Place your goal steps along a time continuum to create milestones that mark your progress and work toward reaching each milestone within a manageable time frame.

Essential Step Three: Expectant Attitude and Beliefs

Keep an open, expectant attitude as you set goals and place them within the milestones, but don't let your desire to get where you want to go quickly seduce you into setting goals you cannot reach in the time allowed. Think success-success-success. The goals you set need to stretch you, but they also need to be doable.

Until you have all of the essentials in place, lots of things are going to come up that can derail you unless you firmly believe and maintain the positive expectation that you will arrive at your intended destination if you keep correcting your course and moving forward. Clarity and ownership of your ideal life will help here.

From open, expectant attitude and beliefs come the external success drivers of willingness to take risks, forward momentum, and openness to new possibilities.

Essential Step Four: Solid Personal and Relationship Boundaries

With awareness of your authentic self, connection to your passion, a clear and purposeful vision to guide you, and an attitude of positive expectation to fuel motivation, clarity around how you choose to show up in the world begins to develop. As it does, you will need solid boundaries to help you move through life on your own terms. To build those boundaries, you may need to develop some skills you don't now have such as assertiveness, negotiation, and persuasion skills. If you lack any of these skills, spend some time learning the basics so you stay on the path of your choosing and don't lose precious time.

From solid personal and relationship boundaries come the external success drivers of assertiveness, discernment, negotiation and personal power.

Essential Step Five: Self-confidence

This step is not so much a conscious function as it is a result of developing the other steps, but it can be enhanced by familiarizing yourself with the confidence formula (Knowledge + Experience + Positive Feedback) and evaluating any areas where you lack confidence so you can make corrections. Confidence will naturally increase as you develop good, healthy boundaries around a strong sense of self provided you have the knowledge you need. As your confidence increases, your ability to attract the right people and circumstances to speed your progress will increase and your successes will multiply.

From self-confidence comes the external success drivers of winning attitude, persuasion, negotiation, determination, and fearlessness.

Essential Step Six: Self-Esteem

As self-confidence grows and you become more and more certain that you can achieve what you set out to do, your self-esteem will increase. As self-esteem increases and you allow your wants and needs to be just as important as anyone else's, your capacity to achieve your goals and realize your dreams will increase exponentially.

Realize that self-esteem is *not* the same as self-importance. Acknowledging that your desires are *as* important as anyone else's doesn't mean that you are putting yourself above anyone. Just that you aren't putting yourself below anyone. It's a declaration of equality which you will discover serves you very well.

You don't need to worry about becoming snooty or arrogant as self-esteem develops. You will never become arrogant if you have developed your authentic self first. Besides, arrogant people don't really have self-esteem. Arrogance or self-importance is a result of insecurity and *low* self-esteem, not healthy self-esteem. With a healthy dose of self-esteem, you will know your own worth and, when you do, your boundaries will grow stronger and the opinions of others will cease to negatively impact you. Stress will drop, happiness increase, and your ability to self-manage will get easier. At that point, you are well on your way to success.

If you have spent a lifetime putting yourself on a back burner to serve others, you may need to deal with feelings of guilt when you first start putting your own needs first. The best way to deal with that is to remember that you can only give to others what you own. Work on owning happiness and success, so you have more of these to share.

From self-esteem comes the external success drivers of worthiness, faith in self, personal power, sustained progress, self-care, and a sense of equality.

Essential Step Seven: Effective Self-management

Once others cannot impact you negatively, self-management becomes a natural and enjoyable function. And with effective self-management, the beliefs you hold about yourself, others, and the world (your values) will shift in positive ways. You will begin developing healthier relationships and will discover there are lots of people willing to help you. As you allow other healthy people into your life, your options will increase and your successes will increase along with them.

From effective self-management comes the external success drivers of emotional intelligence, personal and interpersonal effectiveness, patience, collaboration, leadership qualities, and wisdom.

There is One More Thing You Must Do…

Though this is presented last, it is not the last step. It's actually the *first* step, and it is a step that you *must* take or you absolutely cannot have lasting success.

That first essential step is to **begin.** Start *right now*, keep at it and enjoy the journey! If you do, the lasting success you dream of having *will* be yours.

If You Need Additional Help

I spent years researching the keys to success and wrote this book because my passion is helping people succeed in the fastest possible way and, although some people see offering additional solutions as a sales gimmick, a book leaves people free to take or leave whatever they choose. But, to choose wisely, you need to know what's available to you and, if I didn't share that with you, I would be doing you a disservice.

Your own strengths and capacities are among the things you have available, so go as far as you can on your own as long as you are making steady progress. Most people are able to navigate life on their own more than 90% of the time. What keeps people stuck are the transition points which they don't have the skills or knowledge to navigate on their own. These make up less than 10% of our experiences, but can eat up 90% of your time if you get stuck there. So, do all you can on your own and, if you get stuck, seek help so you don't lose time or momentum.

Sometimes, people in your immediate circle can help, and you might want to try that avenue first. But to help you transition through the seven essential qualities, it's best to rely on people who are trained to help you develop them. That will be a coach, but not just any coach will be able to help you, especially in the crucially important areas of discovering and developing your authentic self or quickly eliminating mental and emotional blocks. To get the farthest in the fastest possible way, coaches specifically trained to help you develop these and the other essential qualities will be your best bet.

The coaches we train and certify through Quantum Leap University are highly skilled at helping people get where they want to go in the fastest, most effective way possible. They can get you farther in a few hours than most other methods do in months and even years.

So, if you get stuck and need help, please contact my team so we can direct you to the coach best suited to help you reach your particular goals. You can reach us by going to www.quantumleapuniversity.org, selecting "Contact" from the top menu bar, and sending us a contact request.

Or you can select a coach from the "Find a Coach" link in the top menu bar.

You Will Find Four Kinds of Coaches There:

1. **CORE Coaches** who are trained and certified to administer and provide consultation and coaching on the CORE MAP assessment and help you discover and develop your authentic self.

2. **RAMP Coaches** who are trained and certified to facilitate RAMP sessions to help you quickly eliminate subconscious blocks and limiting beliefs in as little as an hour.

3. **Success-GPS Coaches** who are trained and certified to deliver and coach you through the Success-GPS assessment which provides you with a clear picture of what you are doing, or not doing, to get the results you are currently getting so you can focus your efforts on what will get you the results you want.

4. **Quantum Leap Coaches** who are trained and certified to administer and coach around all three of our signature tools: the CORE MAP assessment, the RAMP method, and the Success-GPS assessment. Quantum Leap Coaches can help you discover your authentic self, quickly get past blocks, and coach you through areas of your life that are not working for you so you progress very quickly.

However you choose to get on your own authentic path and travel it, commit to making it happen. Nothing you will ever do will bring you more joy or a more abundant and successful life.

About the Author

Sherry Buffington has been immersed in the study of human nature, motivation and success principles since 1978. She is a pioneer in the field of cutting edge assessments and products which produce exceptionally fast, impressive and lasting results. Her work has taken personal and professional development, and the means for achieving true and lasting success to a whole new level.

Sherry is a psychologist, consultant, coach, trainer, presenter and the founder of two successful companies. She is the originator and co-developer of the highly acclaimed *CORE Multidimensional Awareness Profile (CORE MAP)* and the *CORE Personal Effectiveness Profile (CORE PEP)*, and the creator and developer of the *Rapidly Accelerated Mind Patterning* (RAMP) method and the *Success-GPS* assessment. She is a best-selling author, and has authored several books, including *Who's Got the Compass?...I Think I'm Lost!*, *The Law of Abundance*, and *What Cheese: How to Say What You Mean to Get What You Want*, and co-authored two books on leadership for the new generation workforce, *Exiting OZ* and *Power Shift*. Her products and programs, and her dedication to ensuring fast, effective, measurable results have contributed to the successes of hundreds of organizations and thousands of individual lives.

Visit our websites at:

    www.quantumleapuniversity.org

    www.coremap.com

    www.banishblocks.com

    www.thelawofabundance.com

    www.starperformancesystems.com

    www.fromahigherperspective.com

www.ingramcontent.com/pod-product-compliance
Lightning Source LLC
Chambersburg PA
CBHW020659300426
44112CB00007B/446